LifeLight

"In Him was life, and that life was the light of men." John 1:4

Proverbs

—

LEADERS GUIDE

CONCORDIA PUBLISHING HOUSE • SAINT LOUIS

Proverbs describes Wisdom as a tree of life and blessing to those seeking and taking hold of her teachings (Proverbs 3:18). Wisdom's branches are laden with only the choicest of fruits, yielding a crop of righteousness. This in turn blesses others (11:30). As a tree, Wisdom reminds us of two trees in the Garden: the tree of the knowledge of good and evil, and the tree of life. Through man's foolishness and rebellion, the first tree brought death and separation from God. By dying on a tree, (1 Peter 2:24), Christ opened our way to eat from the second tree: life with God and Christ forever (Revelation 2:7).

Earl H. Gaulke, editor

Written by Ken Schurb and Edward Engelbrecht

Cover illustration by Sarah Hollander © Images.com/CORBIS

This publication may be available in braille, in large print, or on cassette tape for the visually impaired. Please allow 8 to 12 weeks for delivery. Write to the Library for the Blind, 7550 Watson Rd., St. Louis, MO 63119-4409; call toll-free 1-866-215-2455; or visit the Web site: www.blindmission.org.

Manufactured in the U.S.A.

3   4   5   6   7   8   9   10   11   12   25   24   23   22   21   20   19   18   17   16

Contents

Introduction

Welcome to LifeLight

A special pleasure is in store for you. You will be instrumental in leading your brothers and sisters in Christ closer to Him who is our life and light (John 1:4). You will have the pleasure of seeing fellow Christians discover new insights and rediscover old ones as they open the Scriptures and dig deep into them, perhaps deeper than they have ever dug before. More than that, you will have the pleasure of sharing in this wonderful study.

LifeLight—An In-depth Study

LifeLight is a series of in-depth Bible studies. The goal of LifeLight is that through a regular program of in-depth personal and group study of Scripture, more and more Christian adults may grow in their personal faith in Jesus Christ, enjoy fellowship with the members of His body, and reach out in love to others in witness and service.

In-depth means that this Bible study includes the following four components: individual daily home study; discussion in a small group; a lecture presentation on the Scripture portion under study; and an enhancement of the week's material (through reading the enrichment magazine).

LifeLight Participants

LifeLight participants are adults who desire a deeper study of the Scriptures than is available in the typical Sunday morning adult Bible class. (Mid-to-older teens might also be LifeLight participants.) While LifeLight does not assume an existing knowledge of the Bible or special experience or skills in Bible study, it does assume a level of commitment that will bring participants to each of the nine weekly assemblies having read the assigned readings and attempted to answer the study questions. Daily reading and study will require from 15 to 30 minutes for the five days preceding the LifeLight assembly. The day following the assembly will be spent reviewing the previous week's study by going over the completed study leaflet and the enrichment magazine.

LifeLight Leadership

While the in-depth process used by LifeLight begins with individual study and cannot achieve its aims without this individual effort, it cannot be completed by individual study alone. Therefore, trained leaders are necessary. You fill one or perhaps more of the important roles described below.

The Director

This person oversees the LifeLight program in a local center (which may be a congregation or a center operated by several neighboring congregations). The director

- serves as the parish LifeLight overall coordinator and leader;
- coordinates the scheduling of the LifeLight program;
- orders materials;
- convenes LifeLight leadership team meetings;
- develops publicity materials;
- recruits participants;
- maintains records and budgeting;
- assigns, with the leadership team, participants to small discussion groups;
- makes arrangements for facilities;
- communicates outreach opportunities to small-group leaders and to congregational boards;
- follows up on participants who leave the program.

The Assistant Director (*optional*)

This person may assist the director. Duties listed for the director may be assigned to the assistant director as mutually agreeable.

The Lecture Leader

This person prepares and delivers the lecture at the weekly assembly. **(Lesson material for the lecture leader begins on p. 9.)** The lecture leader

- prepares and presents the Bible study lecture to the large group;

- prepares worship activities (devotional thought, hymn, prayer), using resources in the study leaflet and leaders guide and possibly other outside sources;

- helps the small-group discussion leaders to grow in understanding the content of the lessons;

- encourages prayer at weekly leadership-team and discussion-leaders meetings.

The Small-Group Coordinator (optional; the director may fill this role)

This person supervises and coordinates the work of the small-group discussion leaders. The small-group coordinator

- recruits with the leadership team the small-group discussion leaders;

- trains or arranges for training of the discussion leaders;

- assists the director and discussion leaders in follow-up and outreach;

- encourages the discussion leaders to contact absent group members;

- participates in the weekly leadership team and discussion leaders equipping meetings;

- provides ongoing training and support as needed.

The Small-Group Discussion Leaders

These people guide and facilitate discussion of LifeLight participants in the small groups. **(Lesson material for the small-group leaders begins on p. 45.)** There should be one discussion leader for every group of no more than 12 participants. The small-group discussion leaders are, perhaps, those individuals who are most important to the success of the program. They should, therefore, be chosen with special care and be equipped with skills needed to guide discussion and to foster a caring fellowship within the group. These discussion leaders

- prepare each week for the small-group discussion by using the study leaflet and small-group leaders guide section for that session **(see p. 47)**;

- read the enrichment magazine as a study supplement;

- guide and facilitate discussion in their small group;

- encourage and assist the discussion group in prayer;

- foster fellowship and mutual care within the discussion group;

- attend weekly discussion leaders training meetings.

Leadership Training

LifeLight leaders will meet weekly to review the previous week's work and plan the coming week. At this session, leaders can address concerns and prepare for the coming session. LifeLight is a 1½-hour program with no possibility for it to be taught in the one hour typically available on Sunday mornings. Some congregations, however, may want to use the Sunday morning Bible study hour for LifeLight preparation and leadership training. In such a meeting, the lecture leader and/or small-group coordinator may lead the discussion leaders through the coming week's lesson, reserving 5 or 10 minutes for problem solving or other group concerns.

While it requires intense effort, LifeLight has proven to bring great benefit to LifeLight participants. The effort put into this program, both by leaders and by participants, will be rewarding and profitable.

The LifeLight Weekly Schedule

Here is how LifeLight will work week by week:

1. Before session 1, each participant will receive the study leaflet for session 1 and the enrichment magazine for the course. The study leaflet contains worship resources (for use both in individual daily study and at the opening of the following week's assembly) and readings and study questions for five days. Challenge questions will lead those participants who have the time and desire a greater challenge into even deeper levels of study.

2. After the five days of individual study at home, participants will gather for a weekly assembly of all LifeLight participants. The assembly will begin with a brief period of worship (5 minutes). Participants will then join their assigned small discussion groups (of 12 or fewer, who will remain the same throughout the course), where they will go over the week's

study questions together (55 minutes). Assembling together once again, participants will listen to a lecture presentation on the readings they have studied in the previous week and discussed in their small groups (20 minutes). After the lecture presentation, the director or another leader will distribute the study leaflet for the following week. Closing announcements and other necessary business may take another five minutes before dismissal.

In some places some small groups will not join the weekly assembly because of scheduling or other reasons. Such groups may meet at another time and place (perhaps in the home of one of the small group's members). The discussion leader will obtain the leaflets from the director. A congregation may record the lecture given by the lecture leader at the weekly assembly and duplicate it for use by other groups meeting later in the week.

3. On the day following the assembly, participants will review the preceding week's work by rereading the study leaflet they completed (and that they perhaps supplemented or corrected during the discussion in their small group) and by reading appropriate articles in the enrichment magazine.

Then the LifeLight weekly study process will begin all over again!

Recommended Study Resources for Proverbs

The Lutheran Study Bible, St. Louis: Concordia Publishing House, 2009. This resource contains more than 26,000 study and application notes, a most thorough reference guide, and over 90,000 cross-references, as well as a 31,000-entry concordance, maps, charts, and timelines.

The Lutheran Bible Companion, St. Louis: Concordia Publishing House, 2014. This new resource is a highly visual two-volume handbook that welcomes Christians to a deeper explanation of the cultural and historical contexts of the events captured in Scripture and the Apocrypha.

Ehlke, Roland Cap. *Proverbs* (People's Bible Commentary Series). Milwaukee: Northwestern Publishing House, 1992. Reprinted by Concordia Publishing

House, 1993. A comprehensive commentary at the lay level, based on the NIV text. Especially helpful in connecting Proverbs to the New Testament.

Kidner, Derek. *The Wisdom of Proverbs, Job, and Ecclesiastes: An Introduction to Wisdom Literature.* Downers Grove, IL.: InterVarsity Press, 1985. Somewhat critical, but insightful at points. Attempts to place the Book of Proverbs within the context of the rest of the wisdom literature in light of twentieth-century study. For a general readership.

Roehrs, Walter R., and Martin H. Franzmann. *Concordia Self-Study Commentary.* St. Louis: Concordia Publishing House, 1979. This one-volume commentary on the Bible contains more than 950 pages and is tailored for lay use.

Using Overhead Transparencies

Some lecture leaders like to use a computer-generated presentation or transparencies with an overhead projector. Others find this to be more a hindrance than a help. We recommend that you use PowerPoint, an overhead, or a chalkboard to show at least the outline of each lecture.

The Beginning of Wisdom

1 Kings 3–7; Proverbs 1:1–7

Preparing for the Session

Central Focus

"The fear of the LORD is the beginning of wisdom" (Proverbs 9:10). This study of Proverbs starts by examining "wisdom," the wise reign of Solomon, and "the fear of the LORD" in light of the book's initial admonitions to avoid foolishness and seek wisdom.

Objectives

That participants, by the power of the Holy Spirit working through the Word, will

1. be able to describe several facets of the biblical concept of wisdom;

2. appreciate strengths and limitations of the proverb as a form for communicating truth;

3. be able to differentiate the "fear of the LORD" from slavelike fear on biblical grounds and recognize its importance both in the Book of Proverbs and in their lives;

4. want to be wise in accord with the appeals in Proverbs 1.

Note for small-group leaders: Lesson notes and other materials you will need begin on page 47.

For the Lecture Leader

Proverbs does not provide direct historical background about its authors and their setting. Parts of the Book of Proverbs have a miscellaneous character. Further, if we are not careful, the Gospel can be eclipsed in our discussions by the book's intensely practical bent. This course attempts to deal with these challenges in the following ways:

First: Passages from 1 Kings, Deuteronomy, and Psalm 72 will be included to provide the historical and cultural setting of Proverbs.

Second: A portion of the course will be heavily oriented to chapters of the book that are theologically "packed"; for example, chapters 1–2, 8, and 9.

Third: The lectures for Proverbs 10–31 will be organized around themes and subthemes. These themes should help us see New Testament and Gospel connections more so than if we would try every week to summarize the multiplicity of points from the middle to the end of Proverbs.

Fourth: This course will obviously not treat each proverb. At its end, we want participants to use Proverbs for everyday life situations. Such an aim requires (1) familiarizing students with the major themes of the biblical book at hand, and (2) helping them to understand how this ancient book communicates its message so they can read it themselves with greater effectiveness.

Prepare yourself for your weekly teaching assignment:

1. Pray for the Holy Spirit's blessing upon you for the good of the students as you receive the Word of Life and pass it along to them.

2. Week by week during the course, read for yourself the weekly assignment and all the passages from Proverbs (and elsewhere in Scripture) that are mentioned in the lectures.

3. In addition to your reading for specific class preparation, challenge yourself to read through Proverbs weekly both during the time leading up to the class and while it is going on. You might be surprised at the connections you will see by the end of the course.

Session Plan

Worship

Begin the session with the hymn and prayer printed in the study leaflet. Accompaniments are available in denominational hymnals, such as *Lutheran Service Book* (refer to hymnal index). See the list of study resources on page 7.

Lecture Presentation

Introduction

Tom Landry coached professional football's Dallas Cowboys for some three decades. But his remarkable career began years earlier, as a star player on the University of Texas football team. Before going to Dallas, Landry was an assistant coach of the New York Giants' championship teams of 1956 and 1957. Of that time, Landry said, "football was my whole life—it was my religion."

Despite his early success, Landry noted that something was lacking in his life. Through the study of Scripture, the Lord showed Landry a better way (from *The Concordia Pulpit for 1982* [St. Louis: CPH, 1981], 246–47).

Whether you feel like a success or a failure, this Life-Light course will show you a better way. It focuses on a biblical book that deserves much more attention than it often gets: Proverbs. No other Old Testament book addresses itself to human attitudes and insights for life quite like Proverbs. It tells us that any picture of life in which the Lord God has been left out, or relegated to a small part on the side, is desperately wrong. Proverbs shows us a better way: the way of wisdom. (1:1–2) "The proverbs of Solomon son of David, king of Israel" are "for attaining wisdom."

1 Wisdom

The story is told of an atheist who kept a Bible in his desk drawer. His explanation? "That Book of Proverbs has so much wisdom in it." In purely secular terms, people respect wisdom. They realize that it is not mere knowledge of data. A person is wise who can discern how to deal with other people, conditions, or situations well. A wise person can correct what is wrong, get the best out of the worst, and judge with fairness and accuracy.

In some places Scripture speaks of wisdom as fairly ordinary. For example, those who made Aaron's priestly garments had wisdom (see Exodus 28:3). The Book of Proverbs does not teach professional skills, but much of its wisdom is intensely oriented to the practicalities of life.

There is more, though. Wisdom can include God's Law. Or it can include relating with God and fitting into the scheme of His mighty acts.

Biblical "wisdom" ranges across all these aspects and still more besides, as we shall discover later. It teaches that God is at work in life's ordinary things. It sees God steadily and sees Him whole. It sees God in every aspect of life, in both good and bad.

At the time of Moses God guided His people's lives through detailed laws of holiness. At the time of Solomon and the other kings of Israel, God spoke to His people through "wisdom literature" like Proverbs, to guide them in the way of life. They could "see" something of the Lord and His ways in the historical books. They could "hear" from the prophets. But books like Proverbs helped them to *understand.*

Do we need understanding any less? Coach Landry would say no. We need wisdom perhaps more now that ever. We need to distinguish success from profit. We need to distinguish what we can do from what we ought to do. We need to focus on "whatever is true, whatever is noble, whatever is right, whatever is pure, whatever is lovely, whatever is admirable" (Philippians 4:8). Only divine wisdom can see the gems of goodness amid the glittering shards of destruction brought by sin.

2 "The Fear of the Lord"

In Proverbs 1:7, "The fear of the Lord" is called "the beginning of knowledge." This is the theme verse of Proverbs. A bit later, Proverbs 9:10 says, "the fear of the Lord is the beginning of wisdom."

In the Book of Proverbs, "the fear of the Lord" is paralleled with "the knowledge of God" (2:5) or "knowledge of the Holy One" (9:10). It is the opposite of despising wisdom (1:7). Being wise in one's own eyes, hating knowledge, pride, arrogance, evil behavior, and perverse speech are all set in contrast to "the fear of the Lord," along with being devious, envying sinners, and hardening one's heart.

But what, precisely, does it mean to *fear* the Lord? To cower before Him and wish to escape from Him? *Fear* certainly can have this meaning, sometimes called "slavelike fear." Unquestionably, in the Book of Proverbs the Lord is one to be reckoned with.

The "fear of the LORD" is more than slavelike fear. It is "childlike." The Bible associates "the fear of the LORD" with forgiveness and salvation:

> Surely His *salvation* is near those who *fear* Him." (Psalm 85:9)

> "With You there is *forgiveness;* therefore You are *feared.*" (Psalm 130:4)

Proverbs extends this theme: (14:26–27) "He who fears the Lord has a secure fortress, and for his children it will be a refuge. The fear of the Lord is a fountain of life, turning a man from the snares of death."

Sinners can have such confident fear of God only because of Jesus Christ. The people who first heard the proverbs had also heard about the coming Messiah who would be their Savior: Eve's Offspring who would crush the devil's head, the Seed of Abraham in whom all the nations of the earth would be blessed, the Prophet like Moses who would bring a better message than that of Moses, the Sufferer whose hands and feet were pierced as He was forsaken by God, the Holy One whom God would not abandon to the grave, the Son of God (Genesis 3:15; 22:18; Deuteronomy 18:15–18; Psalm 22:1, 16; 16:10; 2:7). The fear of the Lord, taught by the Word of the Lord, sees God's promise of salvation amid the displays of His power. The world may nod its head toward God's glory and say, "Your Majesty!" The child of God, by contrast, bows his or her head and says, "My Majesty and my Savior." Christ's saving work forms the reason why the fear of the Lord can be the beginning of wisdom, not the token of death.

Our hearts fear God on account of sin. But because of God's forgiveness and salvation in Christ our fear can be that of a child and heir, rather than that of a slave. It is the fear of a forgiven sinner.

A house fire trapped a little boy in his second-story bedroom. From outside, his father called, "Andy, jump out the window. I'll catch you." Through the smoke, the boy cried: "I can't see you, Daddy." His father replied, "That's all right, son. I can see you. Jump!" The boy said, "Just don't go away, Dad!" (Adapted from Donald L. Deffner, *Seasonal Illustrations for Preaching and Teaching* [San Jose: Resource Publications, 1992], 141.)

Slavelike fear is the fear that God will come. Childlike fear is the fear that He will go away.

With childlike fear, Andy could go through his window, for he had an escape from the fire and safety in his dad's arms. The Book of Proverbs says, (19:23) "The fear of the LORD leads to life." With this fear we can go safely through the world, escaping its many dangers.

Conclusion

Through the last question on your study sheet you discovered that Proverbs is not one book written by Solomon but a collection of books probably written and collected by a number of people. Keep these various collections of proverbs in mind as you study. Also keep Solomon in mind as the chief author and collector. Look for contrasts between what Solomon wrote and what he did.

Although Solomon was the wisest man who ever lived, he still stumbled and sinned. His warnings often echo his personal regrets. What parent hasn't said "Don't!" about something they did in their youth! The opening chapters of Proverbs read like a personal confession of this fallen king. When the wise men of Hezekiah combed through Solomon's many sayings more than 200 years later to make their own collection, they left out his words about cedars and hyssop, animals and birds, reptiles and fish. But they had to include these wise words: (Proverbs 28:13–14) "He who conceals his sins does not prosper, but whoever confesses and renounces them finds mercy. Blessed is the man who always fears the LORD."

Through the study of God's Word, Tom Landry also grasped these truths. His life—lived by God's wisdom—inspired and encouraged his players and fans. It won him broad respect among believers and nonbelievers alike. These are some of the blessings that come with wisdom. But the greatest blessing is the Lord Himself, who is the first and the last. He hears our cry for wisdom and answers not in words alone but in person, the person of His Son, Jesus Christ. Through forgiveness in Christ we learn not just to fear the Lord but also to love Him. To fear Him is the beginning of wisdom. To love Him is the goal (Deuteronomy 6:5).

Concluding Activities

Make any necessary announcements. Distribute the enrichment magazine and encourage participants to read it as part of their weekly study. Then distribute study leaflet 2.

The Way of Life and the Way of Death—Part 1

Proverbs 1:8–3:35

Preparing for the Session

Central Focus

"Trust in the LORD with all your heart and lean not on your own understanding; in all your ways acknowledge Him, and He will make your paths straight" (Proverbs 3:5–6).

Objectives

That participants, by the power of the Holy Spirit working through the Word, will

1. be able to contrast the way of wisdom with the way of folly as to their characteristics and their outcomes;

2. value the way of wisdom and want to avoid the way of folly.

Note for small-group leaders: Lesson notes and other materials you will need begin on page 49.

For the Lecture Leader

Hearing God's Word affects our living. But living can affect our hearing too. We can never improve upon God's Word, so the effect of our living upon our hearing can turn out negative. Jesus spoke of the seed of God's Word that falls among thorns. This picture "stands for those who hear, but as they go on in their way they are choked by life's worries, riches and pleasures, and they do not mature" (Luke 8:14).

The participants in this LifeLight course are probably all Christians. Still, they have a lot to learn from this week's lesson as it contrasts the way of wisdom with the way of folly. You do too.

Hold your head up as you prepare and teach this week! For as enticing as the way of folly can be, the advantages and inducements of the way of wisdom are far better.

Session Plan

Worship

Begin the session with the hymn and prayer printed in the study leaflet. Accompaniments are available in denominational hymnals, such as *Lutheran Service Book* (refer to hymnal index).

Lecture Presentation

Introduction

A ship's engine stopped running just as a big storm came blowing in. One woman anxiously ran up to the captain and asked, "Is there any danger?" He answered, "Madam, we must trust in God." "Oh," she moaned, "has it come to that?" (Donald L. Deffner, *Windows into the Lectionary* [San Jose: Resource Publications, 1996], xxi).

Forgetting or refusing to trust in the Lord is foolish. Trusting in Him is the way of the wise. One of the most important words in Proverbs is *derek*, usually translated "way" or "path." It occurs 71 times in Proverbs and is applied to both the righteous and the wicked. As you read the first nine chapters of Proverbs, picture yourself at a fork in the road. On one pathway Folly beckons. On the other, Wisdom calls. The way of life and the way of death stretch out before you.

Chapters 1–7 of Proverbs contain 10 appeals or entreaties to follow the way of wisdom, in which the believer should walk each day. Proverbs constantly contrasts the way of the righteous with the way of fools. As one student of the book put it, "Every conceivable literary device is used to make the black appear jet black and the white, snow white; the wise man never concerns himself with grays."

1 Becoming Wise: The Setting

The place to gain wisdom initially is in the home. Near the beginning of the Book of Proverbs, the first of the 10 exhortations to wisdom begins: (1:8) "Listen, my son, to your father's instruction and do not forsake your mother's teaching." Among the proverbs collected later in the book are these: (13:1) "A wise son heeds his father's instruction" and (15:5) "a fool spurns his father's discipline." Proverbs emphasizes the role of parents as teachers, in instruction and discipline and also by example.

In the home, wisdom can be instilled early on. When the reformer Martin Luther gave up celibate life by marrying and becoming a father, he began to consider anew the role of Christian parents and the learning children needed. He recognized how valuable the Book of Proverbs could be to families. He wrote of how wise Solomon "amid so many royal duties . . . still undertook to be a teacher, and particularly—as was most needful—to teach and train young people in the way they should act acceptably before God, according to the spirit, and wisely before the world, with body and possessions . . . This book, therefore, ought early to be impressed on the young people throughout the world and put into daily use and practice" (LW 35:262).

The young learn not only at home but also from their teachers. Sometimes a teacher in the ancient world referred to a student as "my son"; therefore some of these expressions in Proverbs may be the address of a teacher to a pupil instead of a parent to a child. In any case, the book takes it for granted that a child is going to have wise and diligent teachers. In Proverbs 5, a man who has fallen for a wicked woman looks back in regret years later, saying: (vv. 12–13) "How I hated discipline! How my heart spurned correction! I would not obey my teachers or listen to my instructors" (see also Proverbs 15:12).

In our experience, teachers typically have textbooks. Even in antiquity, when actual books were rare, there was still a core of material to be passed on—as in a textbook today. "The sayings . . . of the wise" were handed down by memorization and repetition (Proverbs 1:6; see 22:17; 24:23). Similarly, Proverbs elsewhere refers to the "words of knowledge" (19:27; 23:12). However, "a proverb in the mouth of a fool," simply repeated but not understood and appreciated, is likened to "a lame man's legs that hang limp" and "a thornbush in a drunkard's hand" (26:7, 9). It is useless and even potentially harmful. The wise both remember and reflect upon wise words. Like Solomon, they pray for wisdom.

This can be done anywhere.

There are many opportunities to learn wisdom. As in Proverbs 1, so also in Proverbs 9, wisdom is anything but hidden. From the highest point in the city, the invitation of wisdom goes out (9:3; compare 1:20).

2 Warning: Enticement

A contest in England once asked what was the shortest way to travel from Liverpool to London. The winning answer was to travel with "good company."

God made humans social creatures. He made us to depend on one another and interact. But it is important to recognize that temptations can come to us through socializing. What we regard as "good company" can leave us in very bad places. A secular proverb tells of the effect of bad company on good morals. The Book of Proverbs teaches similarly: (13:20) "He who walks with the wise grows wise, but a companion of fools suffers harm."

At the beginning of Proverbs "my son" is warned that sinners should not make a fool of him. While the wise walk in God's way, fools do the opposite. The Book of Proverbs is filled with an awareness of sin. (20:9) "Who can say, 'I have kept my heart pure; I am clean and without sin'?" Obviously, no one can say so, even though some sinners are more open and notorious than others.

In Proverbs 1:11–14, notorious sinners plot to ambush and murder for financial gain. Their greed prevents them from seeing that "they waylay only themselves" (1:18). Birds are not so stupid as to walk into a fatal trap, but fools entangle themselves (1:17).

A word to the wise is sufficient. Ill-gotten gain "takes away the lives of those who get it" (1:19). Don't lose your wisdom and join them.

3 Warning: Don't Reject Wisdom

In the rest of Proverbs 1, wisdom is pictured as calling out to people in the most populated parts of a town: (v. 22) "How long will you simple ones love your simple ways?" If they would have listened, (v. 23) "I would have poured out my heart to you and made my thoughts known to you." But they rejected her when she called and ignored all her advice. Wisdom retorts,

(v. 26) "I in turn will laugh at your disaster." Elsewhere in Scripture, (Psalm 37:13) "the Lord laughs at the wicked, for He knows their day is coming."

It may be difficult to picture the Lord and wisdom taking delight in the slapstick fall of the wicked. Taking pleasure in the pain of others seems inappropriate, since a later Proverb states, (24:17–18) "Do not gloat when your enemy falls; when he stumbles, do not let your heart rejoice, or the LORD will see and disapprove and turn His wrath away from him."

However, we should remember that the Lord looks beyond the ridiculous circumstances fools create for themselves. The Lord sees the lessons people learn through such falls and, no doubt, He smiles. As the Lord explained to Ezekiel, (33:11) "I take no pleasure in the death of the wicked, but rather that they turn from their ways and live. Turn!"

Proverbs 1:29—Wisdom is available to all, but only on particular terms. People must fear the Lord to have wisdom. Verses 30–31—Those who turn from the Lord and His wisdom will experience the bitter end of foolishness. Verse 32—Fools destroy themselves. Verse 33—Wisdom concludes, "Whoever listens to me will live in safety and be at ease, without fear of harm."

4 You Need Wisdom

Chapter 2 contains an appeal to follow wisdom. The first verse calls attention to God's "commands," referring to all His teachings (see Matthew 28:20). A person is to treasure these words and search for wisdom as for a valuable commodity (see Matthew 6:33). Proverbs 2 announces, *if* one seeks wisdom based on God's Word, *then* (1) (v. 5) "you will understand the fear of the LORD and find the knowledge of God," (2) (v. 9) "you will understand what is right and just," (3) (vv. 12–15) you will be saved by wisdom from the ways of the wicked (vv. 16–19) adulteresses, and (4) (vv. 20–22) "you will walk in the ways of good men."

As mentioned a moment ago, wisdom is available to all but only on particular terms. Proverbs 2 reinforces this point. Verse 6 says, "the LORD gives wisdom." Similarly, the New Testament says, (James 1:5) "If any of you lacks wisdom, he should ask God, who gives generously to all without finding fault, and it will be given to him."

God gives wisdom. If He didn't, no one could be wise. For "the wise man is as little wise in and of himself as the righteous man is righteous in and of himself" (O. Weber, *Bibelkunde des Alten Testaments*, 9th ed., tr. Martin H. Franzmann [Hamburg: Furche Verlag, 1961], 330). As we have seen, the beginning of wisdom is the fear of the Lord—that is, fear tempered by faith in God's grace and mercy. Such faith is a gift.

One of the paradoxes of Proverbs is that people can and should pursue wisdom, but finally wisdom remains God's gift. As we pursue wisdom through the study of God's Word, He gives us wisdom first by giving us Christ. Though wisdom gives much practical advice, remember that such insight of itself does a person little good! Proverbs has more than this life in view, as Solomon says: (15:24) "The path of life leads upward for the wise to keep him from going down to the grave."

This is just the reason Christ walked among us, to seek and to save the lost and grant them life everlasting.

5 The Appeal in Chapter 3

Proverbs 3 is the third appeal. After a brief introduction emphasizing the importance of wisdom's teaching, there are several commands, each two verses long, centering on submission to God.

One of the most famous passages in Proverbs is in verses 5–6, which forms a good commentary on the "fear of the LORD" without mentioning that phrase. "Trust in the LORD with all your heart and lean not on your own understanding; in all your ways acknowledge Him, and He will make your paths straight." When the well-known missionary David Livingston was asked how he could do his work in Africa, he responded by quoting these verses. The trusting relationship with God that they depict is not something sinners do by their own reason or strength. It is brought about by God Himself. He was in Christ reconciling the world to Himself, that is, not counting our sins against us. He sent the message of reconciliation into the world through His church (2 Corinthians 5:19–20).

Fearing the Lord, the wise do not consider themselves wise. (Proverbs 3:9) They honor Him with their wealth, for He gives everything. (Verse 8) He takes care of their bodily sustenance, and (v. 12) does not omit discipline. The New Testament quotes verses 11 and 12, underscoring the point that the LORD's discipline of His faithful is a father's discipline (Hebrews 12:5–6). (Hebrews 12:8) "If you are not disciplined . . . , then you are illegitimate children and not true sons." Such discipline is intended not to break our faith, so to speak, but to make it. We Christians can receive God's discipline as that of a father because His Son, Jesus Christ, died and rose for us as our Brother.

Proverbs 3:13 focuses on the basis for a life of submission to God: wisdom. The word *blessed* occurs as the first word in verse 13 and the last in verse 18. This device marks off a section. The word *blessing* would remind the Israelites of a famous biblical contrast: the blessings and curses God promised in the covenant. To be blessed meant more than to be happy. The Hebrew word for "bless," *barak*, literally means "to bend the knee." A Hebrew would bless his or her master by kneeling in adoration. Hebrew masters blessed their servants by laying their hands on them and telling them the benefits of their relationship. The blessing of Jacob and Esau by their father Isaac (Genesis 27) gives a perfect example of this process. The father-son relationship depicted in Proverbs 1–7 corresponds beautifully with this understanding of blessing. By teaching wisdom, the father bestows on his son the means by which he will receive not just material benefits, but most important, the benefits of God's covenant. Those who have wisdom are indeed blessed, for wisdom is better than wealth (3:13–16). Reminiscent of the Garden of Eden, 3:18 calls wisdom a "tree of life." Wisdom gives life, as well as riches and honor (3:16). Personified wisdom has qualities of God Himself. In fact, "by wisdom the LORD laid the earth's foundations" (3:19).

The rest of Proverbs 3 discusses the manner in which the committed life manifests itself. (Verses 21–26) It translates into security for oneself. (Verses 27–32) It also results in wise treatment of others.

There are two ways, those of wisdom and of folly. Verse 33—The Lord blesses the one but curses the other. Even as wisdom laughs at the disaster of fools (see 1:22), so the Lord (3:34) "mocks proud mockers but gives grace to the humble." This verse is quoted by both Peter (1 Peter 5:5) and James (4:6). Peter cites it to warn against pride, while James revels more in its promise of grace.

Conclusion

Like the wise captain in the introduction, Solomon urges you to trust in God. It has "come to that," for whether you see skies that are blue or pitch black, the Lord urges you to live by His wisdom. Solomon began his reign with wisdom. He experienced excellent conditions for economic growth, peace, and glory during his reign. But despite these good conditions his life ended up on the rocks. The siren song of folly and the rocks of sin and temptation threaten you no less. Even though you steer your course in the way of wisdom today, folly will still be there to entice you tomorrow.

Trust in the LORD. With holy wisdom and righteous purpose He will guide you safely. Each day He will meet you at the crossroads of life and point you toward the way of the cross, the way of life under the blessing of His cross. He knows the paths of righteousness like no other. He walked that way some 2,000 years ago and has led millions of other people since. (Proverbs 3:5–6) "Trust in the LORD will all your heart and lean not on your own understanding; in all your ways acknowledge Him and He will make your paths straight."

Concluding Activities

Make any necessary announcements. Ask whether participants are enjoying the enrichment magazine. Continue to encourage participants to read it as part of their weekly study. Then distribute study leaflet 3.

The Way of Life and the Way of Death—Part 2

Proverbs 4:1–8:21

Preparing for the Session

Central Focus

"Listen, my son, accept what I say, and the years of your life will be many. I guide you in the way of wisdom and lead you along straight paths" (Proverbs 4:10–11). God is most important in the lives of wise people. This lesson focuses upon the relationship of the wise with the just and gracious Lord, who speaks both judgment and mercy in the Book of Proverbs.

Objectives

That participants, by the power of the Holy Spirit working through the Word, will

1. identify the appeals from wisdom;

2. learn to avoid common temptations and pitfalls;

3. receive assurance of God's forgiveness for past and present failures.

Note for small-group leaders: Lesson notes and other materials you will need begin on page 51.

Session Plan

Worship

Begin the session with the hymn and prayer printed in the study leaflet. Accompaniments are available in denominational hymnals, such as *Lutheran Service Book* (refer to hymnal index).

Lecture Presentation

Introduction

In a scene from Graham Greene's novel *The Man Within*, a negative, indifferent sort of man becomes angry with his girlfriend for not yielding to him before marriage. She tells him, "'You can't understand. It's not what I call respectability. It's a belief in God. I can't alter that for you. I'd leave you first.'

"'What has he done for you?'

"Her candor was evident to him in the manner in which she met his challenge. She did not sweep it aside in a rush of words as some pious women might have done. She was silent, seeking an answer . . . and at last with a faint note of apology she brought out the brief reply, 'I am alive'" (quoted in *The Concordia Pulpit for 1977* [St. Louis: CPH, 1976], 30).

God the Father, Son, and Holy Spirit creates life, redeems life, and renews life within us. With this God in the middle of our lives we are and remain truly wise.

1 The Three Appeals in Chapter 4

In the previous lecture we examined the first three appeals to wisdom. This lecture covers another seven appeals through the close of chapter 7. It also introduces Proverbs 8–9, which are also written as a series of appeals from wisdom and folly.

Proverbs 4 includes three brief appeals to follow wisdom's way. In the first, Solomon speaks with nostalgia: (vv. 3–4) "When I was a boy in my father's house, still tender, and an only child of my mother, he taught me." We know that Solomon had prayed for wisdom to lead God's people (2 Chronicles 1:7–13; see 1 Kings 3:3–28). But here we get a glimpse of how he learned wisdom from his father, King David, the man after God's own heart. No wonder Solomon was able to speak 3,000 proverbs (less than a third of which are compiled in the Book of Proverbs, by the way). He also had 1,005 songs (1 Kings 4:32).

Already during Solomon's youth, David had impressed upon him the need for wisdom. (Proverbs 4:5) "Get wisdom, get understanding," David said. The language is that of purchase, as a bridegroom would make a payment to his future father-in-law for his wife. The place of wisdom in a believer's life is not purely intellectual. Rather, (vv. 6–8) "love her, and she will watch over you. . . . Esteem her, and she will exalt you; embrace her, and she will honor you." Wisdom wins a person's allegiance.

Verses 10–19—The next appeal includes perhaps the most pointed contrast in the book between the way of wisdom, where the righteous walk, and the way of folly, where fools are found. Verse 19—The wicked live in darkness. Verse 16—They cannot sleep unless they do some sort of wrong. Verse 18—But "the path of the righteous is like the first gleam of dawn, shining ever brighter till the full light of day."

Verses 20–27—The next appeal is the shortest of the 10. It refers to human bodily senses and body parts in order to give a total picture of what wisdom does for the wise. Wisdom claims their ears, eyes, and hearts. It guides their mouths, eyes, and feet. Here and throughout the Book of Proverbs we encounter figures of speech mentioning body parts. Usually these refer to the whole person but bring a specific characteristic to the fore; for example, (v. 23) "guard your heart, for it is the wellspring of life."

2 The Appeal in Chapter 5

Elsewhere in Proverbs the way of wisdom is called (12:28) the way of righteousness," (5:6) "the way of life," and (10:29) "the way of the LORD." But the way of fools is called an evil path, the way of the wicked and the guilty and of death (see Proverbs 28:10; 2:12; 21:8; 14:12); in short, (16:29) "a path that is not good." So why would anyone follow the way of fools?

Once again, the allure is more than a matter of the intellect. Proverbs repeatedly mentions two enticements to evil. We have already encountered the prospect of wrongful material gain. (Recall 1:10–19.) The other is temptation to sexual sin, personified by the adulteress in chapters 5–7.

This image is important for Proverbs, and also for the Book of Hosea and Ezekiel 16 and 23. Each author describes idolatry as spiritual adultery.

Proverbs 5 begins with a sober warning against underestimating the temptation involved. Commentator Martin Luther observed that in general fools are not called buffoons or simpletons in the Book of Proverbs but rather "all kinds of loose, frivolous, heedless people, and most of all . . . those who live without God's Word, acting and speaking according to their own reason and purpose." Luther summarizes, "when Solomon speaks of fools, he is speaking not of plain or insignificant people, but precisely of the very best people in the world" (LW 35:261). These apparently "fine people" fall into just the kind of temptation described in Proverbs 5. They become spiritual adulterers, if not adulterers with their bodies.

Even the adulteress herself does not realize the depths to which she has sunk. Verse 6—"She gives no thought to the way of life; her paths are crooked, but she knows it not." Later, Proverbs adds, (30:20) "This is the way of an adulteress: She eats and wipes her mouth and says, 'I've done nothing wrong.'" Like all stops on the way of folly, adultery and idolatry only lead to dead ends. After all, the Lord sees everything.

Verses 15–20—The wise person is far better off to stay with his or her spouse, and, yes, enjoy her or his sexuality. The wise are also much better off to continue in the fear of the Lord. Proverbs adds: (28:13) "He who conceals his sins does not prosper, but whoever confesses and renounces them finds mercy." God's mercies are ever new to us in Christ.

3 The Two Appeals in Chapter 6

Proverbs 6 contains two appeals. The first, in verses 1–19, provides a brief break from the theme of sexual purity. Verses 1–5—Initially, it warns about situations into which the naive fall. The young and inexperienced can make foolish financial commitments, such as taking responsibility for the debts of strangers. They are not alone in having a capacity for sloth, but laziness can easily become a trap for them. Verses 6–11—Of "get-rich-quick schemes," Proverbs counsels industry like that of the ant.

Verses 12–15—A more advanced state of foolishness and wickedness is shown by the "scoundrel and villain" of these verses. Disaster will strike him suddenly. Verses 16–19—Then follows a catalog of six, no, seven sins detested by the Lord. This list is rather inclusive. Its items are all mentioned at least once more in Proverbs.

The Lord detests

"haughty eyes,

a lying tongue,

hands that shed innocent blood,

a heart that devises wicked schemes,

feet that are quick to rush into evil,

a false witness . . .

and a man who stirs up dissension."

Most items on this list sound very much like us too. What's wrong with the world? Me. I desperately need God's forgiveness, and so do you. Thank God, He gives it to us in Christ.

The second half of Proverbs 6 contains another appeal to follow wisdom's way. It begins with language similar to what we have encountered before, that one does well to heed wise teachings and to keep them close by: (v. 21) "Bind them upon your heart forever; fasten them around your neck." (See Proverbs 1:9; 3:3–4.) The words resemble the instruction of Deuteronomy 6:6–9 to keep God's Word where it is readily accessible and frequently used.

This is important, for the "immoral woman" is tempting indeed. (Proverbs 6:25) "Do not . . . let her captivate you with her eyes." Compared to Proverbs 5, chapter 6 intensifies both the descriptions of her attractiveness and the utter folly of getting involved with her.

(6:29) "No one who touches her will go unpunished." Verse 34—Obviously, her husband will be furious. (Verses 27–32) In any case, "Can a man scoop fire into his lap without his clothes being burned? . . . a man who commits adultery lacks judgment; whoever does so destroys himself."

4 The Appeal in Chapter 7

This general theme continues into chapter 7, which contains the last of the 10 appeals. It is mostly devoted to a true-to-life story of an adulterous woman and her naive victim. While the appeal at the end of Proverbs 6 was notable for its intensity, Proverbs 7 is almost comical. If we laugh, though, it is not because the story is ridiculous and cannot happen. Instead, we chuckle ner-

vously and self-consciously. For we know that it *can* and *does* happen.

Verses 6–9—The young man in the story comes off as a fool, which is exactly what he is. He was not the only young man on the street at dusk, not even the only "simple" one. But he had put himself in a hazardous place at that time of day, and he was unable to avoid its danger. Verses 10–13—The loud, wily, and wayward woman grabs him and kisses him. Verses 14–20—She begins by mentioning something religious, that she fulfilled her vows. This may sound good, but it turns out that she means, *at best*: "I'm forgiven—now let's sin!" After her seductive speech, given in some detail in verses 14–20, the young man follows her haplessly "like an ox going to the slaughter" (7:21). But, as one commentator put it, "The arrows that will pierce him are not Cupid's" (Ehlke, 69). In one way or another, (v. 23) "it will cost him his life."

Verses 25–27—"Do not let your heart turn to her ways," the chapter concludes. For "her house is a highway to the grave." That is where the way of foolishness and wickedness leads.

Conclusion

The early chapters of Proverbs help us toward wisdom, and so toward humility in the right places. They call upon us to be distrustful of ourselves and to trust in the Lord. (7:1–2) "My son, keep my words and store up my commands within you. Keep my commands and you will live. Guard my teachings as the apple of your eye," that is, the pupil of your eye, which is highly sensitive and very valuable. Storing up and treasuring the teachings of God's Word in faith results in life, that is, a relationship with God, who alone gives life.

A boy was riding a bicycle on a path down a hill. Ahead, he spotted a rock alongside the path. He kept telling himself not to hit the rock. But with his fixed eyes upon it, he ended up hitting that rock dead center. "I should have kept my eye on the path where I wanted to go," he thought, "not on the place where I did not want to go." Proverbs goes into some detail about the way of folly, but not so we become preoccupied with it. Instead, Proverbs urges God's people to avoid the way they do not want to go and stick to the way of wisdom.

The Epistle of James says, (3:17) "The wisdom that comes down from heaven is first of all pure; then peace-loving, considerate, submissive, full of mercy and good fruit, impartial and sincere." This description sounds like Christ. It lists a set of qualities that is in us because we are in Christ. He is the Vine, we are the branches. When we are preoccupied with Him, we grow truly wise. For, as we shall see next time, Christ Himself is truly Wisdom.

Concluding Activities

Make any necessary announcements. Ask whether there are any comments or questions about the enrichment magazine content. Then distribute study leaflet 4.

No Christ, No Wisdom; Know Christ, Know Wisdom

Proverbs 8:22–9:18

Preparing for the Session

Central Focus

Proverbs 8 is about Christ, the Son of God, who with the Father and the Holy Spirit is God from all eternity—this same Christ is identified by Proverbs 8 as the One who became incarnate and lives with us today as our Savior and Lord.

Objectives

That participants, by the power of the Holy Spirit working through the Word, will

1. be able to explain the identification of Jesus as Wisdom in Proverbs 8;

2. confide in Christ as Wisdom who gives wisdom and so much more;

3. be alert to relate Christ to the wise sayings in the rest of Proverbs.

4. be able to distinguish between three main ways of teaching wisdom in Proverbs;

5. desire to go the way of wisdom, not that of folly, in the fear of the Lord.

Note for small-group leaders: Lesson notes and other materials you will need begin on page 53.

For the Lecture Leader

Proverbs 8 forms a high point of biblical wisdom literature. For here we find that, ultimately, Christ Himself is Wisdom. The wisdom literature in the Bible is designed to lead us to Him. He makes us truly wise.

Unfortunately, while this interpretation of Proverbs 8 is the historic view of orthodox Christianity, it is held by only a minority of expositors today. As good a resource as the *Concordia Self-Study Bible* may be, for example, it simply *reports* that Proverbs 8:22–31 has "traditionally been understood as a Messianic prophecy." Its own interpretation identifies wisdom in this passage as "an attribute of God involved with Him in creation" (*CSSB*, 957). Therefore, the largest section of the lecture in this lesson is devoted to Proverbs 8:22–31. It spells out reasons for the traditional interpretation.

This lesson also summarizes the settings and means in which wisdom is taught, and it examines the invitation to pursue wisdom and avoid folly in Proverbs 9. These subjects also provide opportunities to review material from the earlier lessons.

Session Plan

Worship

Begin the session with the hymn and prayer printed in the study leaflet. Accompaniments are available in denominational hymnals, such as *Lutheran Service Book* (refer to hymnal index).

Lecture Presentation

Introduction

Rocket scientist Robert Oppenheimer once said, "The best way to send an idea is to wrap it up in a person." It's easy to understand what he meant. However helpful letters, books, e-mail, and teleconferencing may be, nothing quite compares with the presence of a person who knows exactly what to say and says it with passion.

When God wanted to send wisdom into the world, the "wrapping" was already done, so to speak. While the word *wisdom* has several different dimensions in the Book of Proverbs, as we have seen, at the apex Wisdom is far more than mundane skills, wise human relations, or even God's Law or one's relationship with God. God Himself is Wisdom.

As Proverbs 8 shows specifically, Christ is Wisdom. Therefore, we can say, "No Christ, no wisdom." But "know Christ, know Wisdom."

1 Wisdom's Character

Proverbs 1–7 contained a series of 10 appeals to follow the way of wisdom. Then follow chapters 8 and 9 as a sort of climax to the description of the urgent need for wisdom in the first part of the book.

Verses 1–4—After a brief introduction, Wisdom speaks in most of the verses in Proverbs 8. Wisdom does not lurk about, but stands where people gather and calls out to all the sons of Adam. You might recall a similar picture from Proverbs 1:20–21. (See lesson 1.)

Verses 5–11—Wisdom counsels the simple and the foolish to gain understanding. Wisdom's words are truth. They are not crooked or perverse. They are to be preferred to gold or silver or jewels.

Verses 12–14—"I, wisdom, dwell together with prudence; I possess knowledge and discretion . . . Counsel and sound judgment are Mine; I have understanding and power," says Wisdom. Verses 15–16—In part by establishing and informing governments, Wisdom preserves the world.

Verses 20–21—"I walk in the way of righteousness, along the path of justice," says Wisdom, "bestowing wealth on those who love Me and making their treasuries full." However, Wisdom is not to be sought with ulterior motives, but is supremely worthy of being sought.

In verses 22–31 we come to the clearest statement of a point that applies to Wisdom as depicted throughout Proverbs 8. Here Wisdom is much more than a gift given by God. In this chapter Wisdom is the One in whom the Lord delighted from eternity and with whom God created the universe. That is, the Wisdom of Proverbs 8 is none other than the Second Person of the Trinity, the Son of God before His incarnation. It is important to steer clear of any confusion about the identity of Wisdom in this passage.

2 Eternal Wisdom

The confusion stems from the different ways verse 22 has been translated. Some translators render the verse "The LORD *created* Me at the beginning of His work" (RSV, NRSV; the NIV points in a similar direction, saying: "The LORD brought Me forth as the first *of His*

works"). From this translation an incorrect conclusion may follow, that the "Wisdom" speaking here was the first creature made by God.

In the fourth century, a churchman named Arius drew precisely this conclusion. He held that Wisdom was the first creature God made. It was better than the rest, but a creature all the same. Therefore, Arius concluded, Jesus was not fully God. Arius taught about Jesus that there was a time when He was not. This false teaching, the Arian heresy, caused a major doctrinal controversy at that time.

A better translation of verse 22 is "The LORD already *possessed* Me long ago, when His way began, before any of His works" (NET, God's Word). The Hebrew word *Qanah* basically means to "get" or "possess." It can also be used to speak of birth and family relationships. In short, verse 22 indicates that God the Son precedes the work of creation, including the creation of time.

The next few verses tell us more. In verses 24 and 25 Wisdom declares, "I was given birth" before creation. In verse 23 Wisdom says, "I was appointed from eternity." Jesus Christ is true God, begotten of the Father from all eternity. In a famous Christmas prophecy, the prophet Micah wrote that from Bethlehem would come One whose origins are from of old, from days of eternity (Micah 5:2). Jesus prayed in His High Priestly Prayer: "Father, glorify Me in Your presence with the glory I had with you before the world began" (John 17:5).

To combat misunderstandings of Proverbs 8:22 and other passages, leaders in the early church gathered at the city of Nicaea, in what is modern-day Turkey. They adopted a clear statement of faith that most Christian churches still use today. They described Jesus as "God of God, Light of Light, very God of very God, begotten, not made, being of one substance with the Father, by whom all things were made" (Nicene Creed). That last line is precisely what verse 30 teaches. At the creation of the world, Wisdom was at God the Father's side as a Master Craftsman, participating with Him in the work of creation (see Proverbs 3:19–20).

3 The Other Mistaken Identity— and What the Text Says

While Arius was wrong to think of Wisdom in Proverbs 8 as God's first creature, at least he realized that this Wisdom is a Person distinct from the God the Father. In other words, he did not fall into the second possible mistake about this passage, which is perhaps more common today than the first. The second error is to identify the "Wisdom" speaking in Proverbs 8 as God's own attribute or characteristic of wisdom, and to think that it is simply being portrayed as a person is an elaborate figure of speech called "personification." In personification, animals, plants, or things are described as if they were human beings.

The Book of Proverbs employs this figure of speech at points, to be sure. For example, in chapter 9 folly is personified as a foolish woman. But before we chalk up Wisdom in Proverbs 8 to being another instance of literary personification, we must carefully consider what chapter 8 says about this Wisdom.

How can God's own attribute of wisdom be either "gotten" or "begotten"? The prophet Isaiah wrote, "Whom did the LORD consult to enlighten Him, and who taught Him the right way? Who was it that taught Him knowledge or showed Him the path of understanding?" (Isaiah 40:14). Also, we should not forget that in the previous verses of chapter 8 Wisdom was described as both having wisdom (8:12–14) and giving wisdom (8:10–11). This too would be a strange way to speak about God's attribute of wisdom.

Further, it is important to observe that a book like Proverbs usually employs figurative language to make a quick point in a verse or two. (E.g., "A cheerful heart is good medicine, but a crushed spirit dries up the bones," 17:22.) Occasionally, as in chapter 9, it stretches out the figure of speech for a few verses. But in chapter 8 Wisdom is not only described as a Person but also identified as the speaker of the chapter's words in all but the first three verses. If this were a case of personification, it would easily be the longest and most exceptional one in a book that is not given to lengthy figures of speech.

Finally, the New Testament provides a noteworthy parallel to the text that we have been examining. The "Wisdom of God" in Proverbs 8 is identical with the "Word of God" in John 1, the Word who was God (John 1:1) and who became flesh (John 1:14). Elsewhere in the New Testament, Luke 11:49 says that the Wisdom of God sent prophets, but in the parallel passage, Matthew 23:34, Jesus identifies Himself as the sender.

The best news in the Proverbs 8 description of Christ as Wisdom comes in verse 31. At creation, Wisdom not only rejoiced in God's presence, but was also "rejoicing in His whole world and delighting in mankind." This is the delight that moved Him to come into this world for the salvation of the fallen human race. (Much of this discussion of Proverbs 8:22–31 is based on Ken Schurb and Richard Shuta, *Church Year Bible Studies: Series C, Pentecost 1* [St. Louis: CPH, 1995].)

One last point concerning the identification of Christ as Wisdom in Proverbs 8: Grammatically, the Hebrew word for *wisdom* is feminine. Therefore, some Bible translations consistently refer to wisdom as "she." "But that is not to say wisdom is a woman. At times we use feminine pronouns to personify what is not necessarily female. We might, for instance, point to a ship and say, 'There she is!'" (Ehlke, 74).

4 Wisdom's Benefits

Christians know that Christ is the only way to blessedness. Therefore, it strikes us as no surprise when Proverbs 8 says Wisdom is the only way to blessedness. (8:35) "Whoever finds Me finds life and receives favor from the LORD," says Wisdom.

This favor is God's goodwill and acceptance, which is, of course, based on the saving work of Christ Himself. He "has become for us wisdom from God—that is, our righteousness, holiness and redemption," as St. Paul declared (1 Corinthians 1:30). In Christ "are hidden all the treasures of wisdom and knowledge" (Colossians 2:3). These are not curiosities or bits of mental ammunition with which to amaze our friends and co-workers. They are saving treasures. Wisdom warns: (Proverbs 8:36) "whoever fails to find Me harms himself; all who hate Me love death."

Verses 30–31—When the Lord God made the universe, Wisdom was the Master Craftsman at His side. Wisdom was "rejoicing in His whole world and delighting in mankind." This Wisdom, this Word, became flesh and dwelt among us. We know His name. It is *Jesus*, for He saves people from sin.

A Western eye doctor performed successful surgery on a Middle Eastern king. Then he faced a problem. How much should he charge the king? Charging too little would be taken as an insult. On the other hand, the king would likely be angered if the bill ran too high. So the doctor sent the king a note that said: "The king can do no wrong." The next day, the king's messenger brought the note back along with a check for a huge sum, much more than the doctor would ever have charged (Guido Merkens, *Breakthrough for You* [n.p., 1982], 155).

"The king can do no wrong." We Christians can say these words most sincerely. Christ, our King, *is* Wisdom. He could have done anything He wanted to punish sinners like us, and He would have been just in doing so. But, "delighting in mankind" (v. 31) as He did at creation, He became Man, came into this world, and took upon Himself our guilt. He died to pay for all the results of our wicked foolishness. He rose from the dead to send His message of peace with God out into the world. He delights in you.

The world thinks all this is foolishness. But that fact is nothing new. Despite it, the Gospel of Christ makes us wise in head and heart.

The Gospel is not expressed on every page of Proverbs. But the Christ of the Gospel is Himself Wisdom, integrating all the wise sayings we find in the book. No Christ, no wisdom. Know Christ, know Wisdom!

5 The Methods of Wisdom

Proverbs 9 lists the leading ways of teaching wisdom, as mentioned in the book: (9:7–9) "Whoever *corrects* a mocker invites insult . . . Do not *rebuke* a mocker or he will hate you; *rebuke* a wise man and he will love you. *Instruct* a wise man and he will be wiser still." The three general categories are instruction, rebuke, and correction.

Of the three, instruction comes easiest to a recipient. (Proverbs 19:20) "Listen to advice and accept instruction, and in the end you will be wise." But instruction is no light matter: (19:27) "Stop listening to instruction, my son, and you will stray from the words of knowledge." (13:13; see 19:16) Scorning instruction always carries a penalty.

Rebuke is more intense than instruction. The wise appreciate rebukes and know what to do with them: (19:25) "rebuke a discerning man, and he will gain knowledge" (see also 25:12). Not so with stubborn fools: "A man who remains stiff-necked after many

rebukes will suddenly be destroyed—without remedy" (Proverbs 29:1). Proverbs (17:10) says that "a rebuke impresses a man of discernment more than a hundred lashes [impresses] a fool."

Rebukes are administered in order to make people wise, but they have their best effect among those who are already wise.

The third way to teach wisdom is correction. Like rebuke, corrective measures can prove painful. Proverbs says: (15:10) "Stern discipline awaits him who leaves the path." Yet this discipline is worth it, for "he who hates correction will die."

We sometimes feel this way about the discipline of God. However, we should never forget that (3:12) "the LORD disciplines those He loves, as a father the son he delights in." Christians can receive God's discipline as that of a Father because His Son, Jesus Christ, died and rose for us as our Brother.

Discipline, instruction, and rebuke are not only to impart information. Rather, they guide a whole way of life, the way of wisdom.

Conclusion

A military pilot was shot down in the jungle. He sought help from a friendly native to get him back to his own forces. "I want to go to the coast," he said, and his guide nodded. Into the jungle they plunged. After a while, the pilot wondered exactly where they were headed through all the thick foliage. There was no sign of any kind of trail, no markings whatsoever. He stopped his guide and asked, "Where is the road?" "There is no way," the native said, "I am the way" (from Merkens, 136).

(John 14:6) "I am the way and the truth and the life," Jesus said. "No one comes to the Father except through Me." In Proverbs 8 Jesus, Wisdom Himself, declares: (v. 35) "Whoever finds Me finds life and receives favor from the LORD."

Concluding Activities

Make any necessary announcements. Distribute study leaflet 5.

Wisdom Contrasts Good and Evil

Proverbs 10–15

Preparing for the Session

Central Focus

God's love for us results in our love not only for Him but also for our neighbor. This lesson takes a broad view of the teaching offered by Proverbs on the relationship between the wise and others.

Objectives

That participants, by the power of the Holy Spirit working through the Word, will

1. recognize significant themes in Proverbs;

2. be able to describe the relationship between the Lord and wise people;

3. be able to begin differentiating Law and Gospel in the Book of Proverbs;

4. be able to describe the teaching of Proverbs about the speech and attitudes of the wise;

5. want to conform themselves to wisdom in their attitudes and words;

6. grow in relationship to God and as a wise person.

Note for small-group leaders: Lesson notes and other materials you will need begin on page 55.

For the Lecture Leader

Much of the present lesson correlates to the Eighth Commandment with respect to the lips. Somewhat more loosely, it correlates to the Ninth and Tenth Commandments with respect to the heart. It initiates a series of five thematic lessons that will treat Proverbs 10–31. It ties together some of the themes that have already been encountered in the Book of Proverbs.

Session Plan

Worship

Begin the session with the hymn and prayer printed in the study leaflet. Accompaniments are available in denominational hymnals, such as *Lutheran Service Book* (refer to hymnal index).

Lecture Presentation

Introduction

The first part of Proverbs was organized around the various appeals of wisdom. From Chapter 10 onward the proverbs are organized into various collections. Sometimes it's difficult to see why certain proverbs occur together. At other times some organization can be discerned. In the first part of Proverbs we saw the repeated contrast between two ways. This emphasis on the two ways shapes the presentation of the proverbs in this first collection from Solomon. In chapters 10–15 most of the proverbs are contrasts, continuing the theme of the two ways in their style. But instead of focusing on the structure of these collections, this presentation will consider important themes in Proverbs.

1 Relationship with God

(15:9) "The LORD detests the way of the wicked but He loves those who pursue righteousness." Just as the word *wisdom* can have different meanings, so can *righteousness*. Much of the time, Proverbs uses *righteousness* in the sense of "civic righteousness," doing good in the world. But at points the book refers to the righteousness that alone can serve as the bedrock for a sinner's relationship with God, the righteousness given by God Himself due to the obedient life and sacrificial death of Christ.

Chapter 11 contains several proverbs on the value of righteousness. (11:5) "The righteousness of the blameless makes a straight way for them," it says, "but the wicked are brought down by their own wickedness." Similarly, (11:6) "The righteousness of the upright delivers them, but the unfaithful are trapped by evil desires." Within the total context of the Book of Proverbs, it is impossible for the righteousness mentioned in these verses to be self-righteousness, a righteousness that a person might attain apart from God's gift of wisdom. For faithful people are simply not to be found in this world; no one is clean and without sin. (See Proverbs 20:6, 9)

Proverbs 11 indicates that righteousness is sometimes bigger than the capability of sinful men and women. (11:7, 4) "When a wicked man dies, his hope perishes," but "righteousness delivers from death." Who can effect such a rescue but God Himself? Elsewhere, Proverbs says: (14:32) "Even in death the righteous have a refuge." They run to the name of the Lord and are safe, as if they occupied a strong tower (18:10). In these expressions, then, the Lord Himself is their Righteousness, their refuge from sin and death. As a result, (12:28) "In the way of righteousness there is life; along that path is immortality," for (10:29) "the way of the LORD is a refuge for the righteous." Likewise, (15:24) "The path of life leads upward for the wise to keep him from going down to the grave."

The way for the righteous—as well as the wise—to be related to God is by faith. (29:25) "Fear of man will prove to be a snare," says a proverb toward the end of the book, "but whoever trusts in the LORD is kept safe." (Compare with Proverbs 10:25.) The well-known passage from Proverbs 3 says, (vv. 5–6) "Trust in the LORD with all your heart and lean not on your own understanding; in all your ways acknowledge Him, and He will make your paths straight." While Proverbs does not go into lengthy detail on the fact that sinners receive the righteousness of God through faith in Christ, it attests that faith in the Lord results in security and in being saved from one's own crooked ways.

A person with faith in God prays to God asking (as in the Lord's Prayer!) not for wealth or poverty but for daily bread. (30:8–10) "Give me only my daily bread. Otherwise, I may have too much and disown you and say, 'Who is the LORD?' Or I may become poor and steal, and so dishonor the name of my God." (Also on the subject of prayer, see Proverbs 15:8, 29.)

One of the Lord's blessings upon those who are related to Him by faith is long life. As noted earlier, Proverbs is not silent about the hope of God's people beyond death, but it has still more to say about their longevity in the here and now. (10:27) "The fear of the LORD adds length to life, but the years of the wicked are cut short." The first few chapters of Proverbs repeatedly proclaimed that to follow wise teaching would prolong one's years. (See Proverbs 3:2, 16; 4:10.) Bear in mind that this is a sweeping statement, not applicable in every case. The initial chapters of Proverbs also indicate that so-called innocent people can die prematurely. (See, for example, Proverbs 1:11; 6:17.) Nonetheless, when the faith-

ful remain in ways of obedience, they receive temporal blessings from the creative hand of the Lord where He has determined to give them within His creation. Generally, (16:20) "Whoever gives heed to instruction prospers, and blessed is he who trusts in the LORD."

2 Gossip

During World War II the British began to wonder whether one of their military officers was, in reality, a Nazi spy. To find out, they held an informal gathering. They positioned their suspect so he could clearly see the door by which everyone was entering. Suddenly, in walked a man wearing a full dress German army uniform, shouting, "*Achtung!*" Immediately the suspected man jumped up, clicked his heels, and stood at attention (Wendell Mathews, ed., *Images of Faith* [St. Louis: CPH, 1963], 41–42).

The lips may deceive, but the heart will be found out. Proverbs provides us wisdom with respect to both. As to the lips, this lesson takes up what Proverbs says about gossip, tact, and lying. And as to the heart, we will discuss the teaching of Proverbs on humility, self-control, and hope.

An important focus in Proverbs is the right use of words. Proverbs repeatedly refers to the tools of speech—the mouth, lips, and tongue—and their abilities to harm or heal.

A small group of people was criticizing an acquaintance of theirs. "He's unusual," one said. "Boy, he's different," added another.

Finally, one person spoke up. "You know, he *is* different. I've never heard him speak ill of an absent friend" (adapted from Deffner, *Seasonal Illustrations for Preaching and Teaching*, 102).

(Proverbs 12:18) "Reckless words pierce like a sword, but the tongue of the wise brings healing."

Gossip provides the energy and the "raw materials" for quarrels so Proverbs says, (26:20) "Without wood a fire goes out; without gossip a quarrel dies down." People who gossip betray confidences and thereby do untold damage to others and even to themselves. (See 11:13 and 25:9–10.) The sayings (18:21) "The tongue has the power of life and death" and (13:3) "he who guards his lips guards his life" form powerful examples of figurative speech, and sometimes they are also quite literally true. Proverbs never allows us to lose sight of the fact that (22:1) "a good name is more desirable than great riches; to be esteemed is better than silver or gold."

The epistle of James says, (4:11) "Anyone who speaks against his brother or judges him speaks against the law and judges it," which is a serious enough matter, but it does not end there. For (4:12) "there is only one Lawgiver and Judge, the one who is able to save and destroy." To spread negative gossip is to find fault with God's Law. Such character assassination amounts to an attempt to impersonate God Himself, but this cannot be done. That is a good thing too, for only our almighty Lord God can save us from our own sin by the death and resurrection of Christ.

3 Tact

One of the most famous passages from Proverbs has to do with tact: (15:1) "A gentle answer turns away wrath, but a harsh word stirs up anger." Likewise, (16:24) "pleasant words are a honeycomb, sweet to the soul and healing to the bones."

But a book full of loving rebukes such as Proverbs does not stipulate that no one engage in plain speaking. Tact requires wisdom, which consists in finding a way to express oneself clearly but gently. The idea is to speak the truth in love. (See Ephesians 4:15.)

Proverbs says, (15:23) "a man finds joy in giving an apt reply." (See Proverbs 25:11.) In short, while wicked gossip packs great power for ill, a fit word can be quite a force too. (25:15) "A gentle tongue can break a bone," says Proverbs.

4 Lying

Proverbs says, (12:13) "An evil man is trapped by his sinful talk, but a righteous man escapes trouble." It insists that (19:5, 9) "a false witness will not go unpunished" (see also Proverbs 21:28). Therefore, (13:5) "the righteous hate what is false."

Proverbs does not engage in the kind of reflections about truth that we sometimes encounter, in which a statement or idea is alleged to be true for one person but perhaps not for another. (12:19) "Truthful lips endure forever," the Book says, "but a lying tongue lasts only a moment." It includes the prayer (30:8) "keep falsehood and lies far from me." In no way can falsehood and lies be good.

God expects us to be truthful, for He Himself is *the* truthful One. (30:6) "Do not add to His words, or He will rebuke you and prove you a liar." What God tells us is true. It can be trusted. Most precious of all is His Gospel message: that Christ answered for every one of our sins before God and lived to tell the tale of forgiveness and life. When we pass this Good News along to others, it is most fitting to say, (15:4) "the tongue that brings healing is a tree of life," even though "a deceitful tongue crushes the spirit."

5 Humility

Proverbs tells us that (16:18) "pride goes before destruction, a haughty spirit before a fall."

Proverbs clearly states the reason why pride proves destructive. It is not just that those surrounding a proud person grow weary of all the boasting and arrogance, and therefore determine to take such a person down a peg or two—or more. A proud heart leads to sin, Proverbs says (21:4). The temptation to which Adam and Eve succumbed was one of pride, the temptation to be like God (Genesis 3:5–6).

But if disgrace comes with pride, then wisdom accompanies humility (Proverbs 11:3). (3:7) "Do not be wise in your own eyes," says one of the appeals to follow wisdom early in Proverbs, "fear the LORD and shun evil."

Therefore, (25:6–7) "do not exalt yourself in the king's presence, and do not claim a place among great men; it is better for him to say to you, 'Come up here,' than for him to humiliate you before a nobleman." (Compare 25:27.) Jesus taught this same lesson to people who angled for the seats of honor at a dinner hosted by a ruler who belonged to the Pharisees. He summed up, (Luke 14:11) "Everyone who exalts himself will be humbled, and he who humbles himself will be exalted" (see Luke 14:1–14).

Jesus Himself lived by these words and died by them. He humbled Himself and became obedient unto death, the death of an accursed sinner on a cross, and therefore God has highly exalted Him. (See Philippians. 2:5–11.) Our humility begins in God-given saving faith, which renders all honor to God simply by receiving the salvation He gives on account of Christ.

Proverbs says that the Lord (3:34) "mocks proud mockers but gives grace to the humble" (see James 4:6). One of His gifts to the humble is self-control.

6 Self-Control

(Proverbs 25:28) "Like a city whose walls are broken down is a man who lacks self-control." A city with fallen walls lies defenseless. In a similar way, "the man who can't control his impulses is constantly in danger of blindly following them and then paying the price" (Ehlke, 255). He is defenseless against himself, for foolishly he neglects to control himself. For example, (12:16) "A fool shows his annoyance at once, but a prudent man overlooks an insult." One who is at peace with God in Christ has been set free to be patient with others. (15:28) "The heart of the righteous weighs its answers."

In Proverbs, three arenas of self-control emerge as particularly important. The first is control over one's own anger. (29:11) "A fool gives full vent to his anger," the Book says, "but a wise man keeps himself under control." In blowing his stack, as it were, the fool hurts those around him in addition to himself. On the other hand, (15:18) "a patient man calms a quarrel." By self-control, a person can help others.

The second arena for self-control to which Proverbs draws special attention is restraint against talking too much, especially when you don't have much to say. (18:2) "A fool finds no pleasure in understanding but delights in airing his own opinions." Conversely, (12:23) "a prudent man keeps his knowledge to himself, but the heart of fools blurts out folly." Proverbs even says, (17:28) "a fool is thought wise if he keeps silent."

The third prominent arena for self-control in Proverbs is in the consumption of alcohol. Alcohol itself is a good blessing from God (see Proverbs 3:10), but it can be misused so easily and with such terrible effects: (20:1) "Wine is a mocker and a brawler; whoever is led astray by them is not wise." It easily leads to poverty (see 23:20–21). Therefore, Proverbs says, (23:31) "Do not gaze at wine when it is red" (see also 23:29–35).

7 Hope

It is a truism among students of Proverbs that the book dwells somewhat more on life in this world than on life hereafter. Yet it shows no lack of awareness that hope is very, very important to life. (13:12) "Hope deferred makes the heart sick, but a longing fulfilled is a tree of life." (10:28) "The hopes of the wicked come to nothing," all right, but "the prospect of the righteous is joy." Hope for tomorrow leads to joy for today. (17:22a) "A cheerful heart is good medicine," Proverbs affirms.

But we are sinners living in a sin-filled world. The term *sabotage* is derived from the French word for a wooden shoe, *sabot*. French factory workers protested the conditions under which they had to work by flinging their shoes into the machinery, bringing production to a halt. The wooden shoe we often cast into the machinery of life is one of attitude (from Deffner, *Seasonal Illustrations for Preaching and Teaching,* 5). In the words of Proverbs, (17:22b) "A crushed spirit dries up the bones."

Thus, we need to trust our trustworthy and gracious Lord God. With Him, even though (15:15) "all the days of the oppressed are wretched . . . the cheerful heart has a continual feast." During the Vietnam War, American prisoners of war were confined to a prison they called the "Hanoi Hilton." One former prisoner said, "I couldn't have made it without Jesus Christ and being able to look up and see Him in some of the trying times."

While most of the attention in Proverbs may go to life in the here and now, the book is lit by the glow of the future. (24:14) "Know also that wisdom is sweet to your soul; if you find it, there is a future hope for you, and your hope will not be cut off." This is the hope we have in Christ.

Conclusion

When a hydroelectric dam was going to be built across a valley, an entire small town had to be relocated. The land on which it sat would be submerged by the waters that the dam was going to hold back. But between the decision to build the dam and actual relocation of the town, several months passed. During that time, every building in the erstwhile pretty little town fell into disrepair. The entire place became an eyesore. One of the townspeople commented, "where there is no faith in the future, there is no work in the present" (Michael P. Green, ed., *Illustrations for Biblical Preaching,* Grand Rapids: Baker Books, 1989), 194).

On the other hand, hope for future life cannot help but make its impact on present-day living. Proverbs is about this impact in the life of God's people who know true wisdom in God's Messiah, Jesus Christ.

Concluding Activities

Make any necessary announcements. Distribute study leaflet 6.

Wisdom Builds a Better Life

Proverbs 16:1–22:16

Preparing for the Session

Central Focus

Love for the neighbor, which results from God's love for us, also manifests itself in our work. Based on Proverbs and other biblical books, this lesson focuses on the wise in their work. "Commit to the LORD whatever you do, and your plans will succeed" (Proverbs 16:3).

Objectives

That participants, by the power of the Holy Spirit working through the Word, will

1. be able to describe the teaching of Proverbs about the wise and their work;

2. be prepared for major challenges in faith and life by constant preparation in the form of daily godly living;

3. thank God for what He has done for them, His workmanship, in Christ and appreciate what it means to be a "little Christ" to others;

4. want to act in accord with wisdom in their daily work.

Note for small-group leaders: Lesson notes and other materials you will need begin on page 57.

For the Lecture Leader

This is another lesson giving specific attention to an aspect of life in which God's love moves us to love our neighbors. It connects most closely with the Seventh Commandment.

Session Plan

Worship

Begin the session with the hymn and prayer printed in the study leaflet. Accompaniments are available in denominational hymnals, such as *Lutheran Service Book* (refer to hymnal index).

Lecture Presentation

The campus pastor began his sermon by saying, "Today I want to speak about the greatest sin on this university campus."

The chapel was hushed.

"The greatest sin on this campus is not beer."

You could have heard a pin drop.

"The greatest sin on this campus is not sex."

Still, there was silence. People were leaning forward in their pews to hear.

"The greatest sin on this campus is . . . procrastination" (Terrence E. Johnson, *Emphasis* 14 (Sept. 1, 1984): 22; quoted in Deffner, *Windows into the Lectionary*, 8).

Work is a fact of life. God arranged it that way. Already before the fall into sin, (Genesis 2:15) "the LORD God took the man and put him in the Garden of Eden to work it and take care of it." It was after the fall that God cursed the ground and told Adam, (Genesis 3:19) "By the sweat of your brow you will eat your food," indicating that work would now be difficult and sometimes painful.

Work is a fact of life. The wise must take it into account. The Book of Proverbs has much to say about such topics as work, the avoidance of work, the manner in which work should be done, the rewards of work, and the conditions under which work takes place.

1 Day by Day

There is simply no substitute for consistent work. Proverbs calls attention to the tiny ant. (6:7–8) "It has no commander, no overseer or ruler, yet it stores its provisions in summer and gathers its food at harvest." Among people, the wife of noble character in Proverbs 31 (v. 27) "does not eat the bread of idleness."

If only everyone were so wise! But people foolishly come up with all sorts of alternatives to work. They love pleasure (21:17), chase fantasies (12:11; 28:19), and lose focus (17:24). They talk a good game, but (14:23) "mere talk leads only to poverty."

Yet the most significant alternative to work in the Book of Proverbs is none of these things. It is sleep. (26:14) "As a door turns on its hinges, so a sluggard turns on his bed," Proverbs says.

This lesson can be applied to the Christian life on a still-broader scale. In the words of the sainted Rev. Dr. Donald Deffner, "your life right now may be on a fairly level road, but it could change drastically tomorrow. Some fantastic challenge may meet you within the next day or two. What will you do? It may be a totally unexpected illness. It may be calamity in your home, in your business. It may be a loneliness or a desperation the likes of which you have never experienced before in your life . . . What will you do? How will you get ready?"

Proverbs indicates that "your best preparation is to give attention to *today*. In the little things of your life today, prepare for the big emergencies tomorrow. On the ordinary road you travel right now, get ready for the mountain tomorrow. In the green pastures and by the still waters gird yourself for the valley of the shadow.

"For when you immerse yourself in the means of grace—God's Holy Word and Sacraments—when you live 'in the LORD,' then when you reach the mountain, the shadow, the emergency, you will be God-possessed. He will dwell in you, and you in Him. Put your trust in the Lord, and you will know how to live in the present. Live by God's grace in the present, and the future will not frighten you" (*The Concordia Pulpit for 1978* [St. Louis: CPH, 1977], 6; emphasis original).

2 The Way of Work

The Book of Ecclesiastes says: (2:24) "A man can do nothing better than to eat and drink and find satisfaction in his work. This too, I see, is from the hand of God." These words summarize much of the teaching on work contained in the Book of Proverbs.

As noted earlier, Proverbs teaches about work and its benefits in part by pointing out the contrast with the sorry state of lazy people. Therefore its criticism of them is quite pointed and often repeated. The lazy miss their

windows of opportunity and end up regretting it (Proverbs 20:4). For obvious reasons, (18:9) "One who is slack in his work" is regarded as "brother to one who destroys." Proverbs 21:25–26—Despite his cravings, he refuses to work. But he craves for more. By contrast, "the righteous give without sparing."

The fact that the heart of the righteous is in the right place, so to speak, forms only one component of the way they work wisely and well in this world. Proverbs 13:11—Instead of pinning their hopes on some windfall to come their way, they gather little by little. Proverbs 21:5—Their work is diligent, not hasty. Proverbs 24:27—It is also methodical and well planned.

A note needs to be added about casting lots, which is mentioned in 16:33 and other proverbs. When you read about casting lots in the Bible, you should not envision games of chance. The Israelites did not cast lots for gambling. They cast lots in order to make decisions, much the way someone today might flip a coin to choose between equal options. In fact, the high priest carried a set of lots called Urim and Thummim, which God commanded him to use in Exodus 28:30. When Solomon states that the decision made by casting lots comes "from the LORD," he means that nothing in life is left to chance or luck. God's providential hand touches everything.

The rewards of work come in several forms. Work yields satisfaction. First this can be said in the sense of one's income, perhaps (see Proverbs 10:4), yet not only in that sense. (13:4) "The sluggard craves and gets nothing, but the desires of the diligent are fully satisfied."(See also 12:14.) Similarly, (15:19) "The way of the sluggard is blocked with thorns, but the path of the upright is a highway." One of the many intangible profits from work is honor; even a servant is honored for his good work (27:18). Another intangible profit is independence and, with it, the opportunity to help others and win their respect. (12:24) "Diligent hands will rule," Proverbs says, "but laziness ends in slave labor."

A missionary in China was just beginning to tell the story of Jesus to a group of people. After he spoke for a bit, they brightened up and responded: "Oh, yes, we knew Him. He used to live here." Surprised, the missionary told them that Jesus lived centuries ago in another land. No, the group insisted. They said, "We knew the man you are talking about. He lived in this village." They led their new friend out to the village cemetery and showed him a grave. It was that of a medical missionary who had lived and worked among them. He served their community, healed within it, and at length died there (adapted from *The Concordia Pulpit for 1987* [St. Louis: CPH, 1986], 3).

We Christians are privileged to be "little Christs" to our neighbors in our work. That is, God gives us the opportunity to reflect the love of the One whose greatest glory was to extend Himself to us and lay down His life for us as our Savior. St. Paul wrote that (2 Corinthians 3:18) "we, who with unveiled faces all reflect the Lord's glory, are being transformed into His likeness with ever-increasing glory, which comes from the Lord, who is the Spirit."

3 Government

Work is never done in a vacuum. Proverbs discusses at some length two related matters that, in part, establish the conditions for work and shape the way in which the fruits of work can be enjoyed, namely, government and justice.

Proverbs refers to government quite concretely. It speaks most often of "the king."

Proverbs says, (24:21) "Fear the LORD and the king, my son." For a good king in a way represents God. (16:12) "Kings detest wrongdoing, for a throne is established through righteousness." However, (29:2) "when the wicked rule, the people groan" and (28:28) "when the wicked rise to power, people go into hiding." Thus, it is important to (25:5) "remove the wicked from the king's presence, and his throne will be established through righteousness." In general, (14:34) "righteousness exalts a nation, but sin is a disgrace to any people" (compare 11:11).

To do his work, a king needs solid information. (29:12) "If a ruler listens to lies, all his officials become wicked." Therefore, (14:35) "a king delights in a wise servant" (compare 22:29). In an interesting twist, Proverbs notes that (25:2) "It is the glory of God to conceal a matter; to search out a matter is the glory of kings." (28:2) It is "a man of understanding and knowledge" who "maintains order."

Clearly, though, the wisdom required by a king goes beyond the simple knowledge of facts. Tyrants lack *judg-*

ment (28:16), not necessarily data. On the other hand, (20:28) "Love and faithfulness keep a king safe; through love his throne is made secure," also through being fair to the poor (29:14).

Kings are to be treated with the utmost of deference and humility. (23:1–3a) "When you sit to dine with a ruler, note well what is before you, and put a knife to your throat if you are given to gluttony. Do not crave his delicacies." From the standpoint of subjects, (25:3b) "the hearts of kings are unsearchable." But in this regard, as always, Proverbs assures us of who is really in control: (21:1) "The king's heart is in the hand of the LORD; He directs it like a watercourse wherever He pleases."

4 Justice

Justice is obviously related to kings. It forms a second factor that establishes the conditions for work and shapes the way in which the fruits of work can be enjoyed.

Justice involves fairness and equity. (24:23–25) "To show partiality in judging is not good," says Proverbs. "Whoever says to the guilty, 'You are innocent'—peoples will curse him and nations denounce him. But it will go well with those who convict the guilty, and rich blessing will come upon them."

Justice is not an easy thing to come by in this world where so many people want to possess things without working for them. (28:5) "Evil men do not understand justice," Proverbs tells us, "but those who seek the LORD understand it fully." For example, (11:1) "the LORD abhors dishonest scales," although such a thing seems a trifle to some people. Justice and righteousness may require contenting yourself only to have a little and to pass up the great gain that can come with injustice, perhaps because at some point you refused a bribe (16:8; 17:23). The prophets and the New Testament would later build on the proverb, (21:3) "To do what is right and just is more acceptable to the LORD than sacrifice" (see Hosea 6:6; Micah 6:6–8; Matthew 9:13; 12:7), for it can involve its own sort of sacrifice.

In the end, of course, (29:26) "it is from the LORD that man gets justice." It is important to note that at this point a mere human way to administer justice differs from God's judgment. Human judgment can only judge by what people have done or not done. God can judge that way too. But He can also count or impute the righteousness of Christ to us, and on this basis He declares sinners "not guilty" or justified in Christ. (See Romans 4:5–6, 23–25; 5:18–19; 2 Corinthians 5:14, 10, 21.)

Conclusion

We hate to see our work go down the drain. We have an investment in it. Sometimes we call it "sweat equity." There is a little bit of us in our work.

So it is with God. He hates to see people go down the eternal drain, because they are the crown of His creation and His greatest concern. Human beings are not a mere hobby for a God who spends most of His time keeping galaxies going in space. He regards us as foremost.

A little boy made a miniature sailboat. He crafted it ever so carefully. Finally, he took it out to the lake for its maiden voyage, but the boat got away from him. He was crestfallen. A few days passed. Then, while walking downtown, the boy spotted his boat in the window of a pawnshop. He ran home, gathered up every nickel and dime he could call his own, and hurried back downtown. Minutes later, he emerged from the pawnshop with the boat in his hand. He looked at it and said, "Now you are twice mine: once because I made you and once because I bought you back."

The work of our Lord Jesus Christ was to buy us back for the One who made us in the first place. The price to purchase a world that had foolishly turned its back on God ran enormously high. Only God Himself could pay it. Christ paid the price for us. He Himself became the price. The blood of Jesus Christ, God's Son, covered the cost in full, with more to spare. For it is the blood of the man who is also God.

Now we belong twice to the Lord: once because He made us and once because He bought us back. (Psalm 100:3) "Know that the Lord is God," the psalmist said. "It is He who made us, and we are His; we are His people, the sheep of His pasture."

His care frees us to work for others. It stretches through all the days of our lives and even beyond. For God is the Master Craftsman who both made us and bought us back. (Remember, the Wisdom of Proverbs 8 is none other than Christ Himself!) He will eventually raise us from the dead. (1 Corinthians 15:58) "Therefore, my dear brothers, stand firm," St. Paul wrote. "Let nothing

move you. Always give yourselves fully to the work of the Lord, because you know that your labor in the Lord is not in vain."

Concluding Activities

Make any necessary announcements. Then distribute study leaflet 7.

The Words of the Wise

Proverbs 22:17–24:34

Preparing for the Session

Central Focus

"Do not let your heart envy sinners, but always be zealous for the fear of the LORD. There is surely a future hope for you, and your hope will not be cut off" (Proverbs 23:17–18).

Objectives

That participants, by the power of the Holy Spirit working through the Word, will

1. understand the relationship between Proverbs and so-called worldly wisdom;

2. recognize God's work through Proverbs and the everyday events of life.

Note for small-group leaders: Lesson notes and other materials you will need begin on page 59.

For the Lecture Leader

This session considers the place of God in our everyday lives and the surpassing value of His wisdom.

Session Plan

Worship

Begin the session with the hymn and prayer printed in the study leaflet. Accompaniments are available in denominational hymnals, such as *Lutheran Service Book* (refer to hymnal index).

Lecture Presentation

Introduction

This collection of proverbs, called "the words of the wise," presents us with a unique challenge. Solomon or another Israelite prophet may have written them. But it's entirely possible that an Israelite collected these sayings from pagan wisdom literature. The challenge is, if these sayings did not come from a prophet of the one true God, but from a pagan, can these sayings still be called God's Word?

1 Truth

Jewish and Christian interpreters have wrestled with this challenge by making an important point about truth. An illustration will help us get their point: One day a Christian went out to dig in his field. As he dug he discovered a nugget of gold. He tucked it in his pocket and began to walk home. Along the way the nugget slipped through a hole in his pocket and fell beside the road. Before long, a pagan came by, spied the nugget, and took it home rejoicing. The question may be asked, Was the gold more valuable when it was found by the Christian or was the gold more valuable when it was found by the pagan? Of course, gold is gold no matter who finds it.

Interpreters of the Bible have made the same point about truth. Truth is truth no matter who finds it. If a pagan by research, by experience, or even by accident discovers a truth, that truth is valuable for all people. It is worthy to be trusted and to be taught. As the early church father Justin Martyr stated, "Whatever things were rightly said among all men, are rightly the property of us Christians" (*Second Apology*, 13).

The collector of the proverbs in chapters 22:17–24:34, as well as other writers of Scripture, felt comfortable quoting the truth in the writings of their pagan neighbors because they understood that all truth comes from God, who is the way, the truth, and the life. He even felt comfortable including the Lord's name with these truths. Indeed, he wants you to study these truths

(22:19) "so that your trust may be in the LORD." There is no such thing as Christian truth or pagan truth or that ever-popular saying you hear today, "That may be true for you but it's not true for me!" Truth is truth and all truth comes from God. If the Holy Spirit inspired Solomon or some other wise man to pluck these truths from the writings of a pagan in Egypt, then praise God, who is the author of all that is true, good, and noble.

2 The Fact of God

As we consider what's true, good, and noble, we should bear in mind another truth about the Book of Proverbs. Solomon and the other writers of Proverbs view faith in one God as a matter of common sense. In an earlier study we read in Proverbs 16:33, "the lot is cast into the lap, but every decision is from the LORD." The writers or compilers of the proverbs see the Lord at work in and through His creation, even in little things like casting lots. They never feel compelled to explain and prove God's existence. God is simply there, guiding all of life. The writers almost always call God by His personal name, the name of the God who brought Israel out of Egypt: Yahweh, the LORD. (See Exodus 3:13–14; 20:3.) The first few verses of Proverbs 16 called Yahweh the Creator and Sustainer of life. Without Him, no human plan comes to articulation, let alone action. (16:4) He "works out everything for His own ends." The proud of heart disgust Him, but He works through the wicked and eventually punishes them.

Previous proverbs had noted that (15:3) "the eyes of the LORD are everywhere, keeping watch on the wicked and the good," and that (15:11) "Death and Destruction lie open before the LORD—how much more the hearts of men!" In light of God's holiness (see Proverbs 9:10; 30:3), Solomon says: (16:2) "All a man's ways seem innocent to him, but motives are weighed by the LORD." He is God, and He sits in judgment. (24:20b) "The lamp of the wicked will be snuffed out" by Him. Proverbs 11:21, 23—He will not let them go unpunished. Their hope will end only in wrath.

God is God and we have to answer to Him. This fact colors our entire life. Once the distinguished British pastor Dr. Leslie Weatherhead told of how he had been invited to visit the gardener at a well-to-do estate. The man had a record of fine work, but recently he had taken to his bed without any apparent medical reason. Dr. Weatherhead found him lying on his bed at noon with the curtains drawn shut. He tried unsuccessfully to strike up a conversation. Finally, when Dr. Weatherhead said something about the reality of God's forgiveness, the gardener blurted out a confession through many tears. "The man had done some very sordid things," Dr. Weatherhead recalled; "I heard him out." Then Dr. Weatherhead pronounced the absolution and reminded him of his Baptism. Dr. Weatherhead went downstairs to say good-bye to the lady of the house. Before he reached the front door to leave, around the corner came the gardener in his work clothes, whistling away (reported in Duane W. H. Arnold and C. George Fry, *Francis: A Call to Conversion* [Grand Rapids, MI: Zondervan Publishing House, 1988], 74–75).

People who know and feel the fact of God desperately need a relationship with God. What does Proverbs have to say about this?

3 Learning to Know God from His Word

The Book of Proverbs repeatedly admonishes us to heed the teaching of the wise and of God. Ultimately, the Lord *is* Wisdom. People should listen to Him. (8:32) "Now then, my sons, listen to Me," He says, "blessed are those who keep My ways."

Trying to hear Him or make sense of His ways in nature and in the events of history can leave us very uncertain. A degree of wisdom can be gleaned there, but as one reflects on these things in light of God's Word, (30:5) "Every word of God is flawless; He is a shield to those who take refuge in Him." The Word God speaks does not lead astray.

Much of God's message in Proverbs comes as advice and command. It tells us what to do and not to do. It is Law. A great deal of the material in the book can be arranged using the Ten Commandments as an outline.

An interviewer once asked a number of people, "What do you think of the Ten Commandments?" The first gasped, "Are you kidding?"

Another said, "Well, I don't take them literally."

With a laugh, someone said, "Rules were made to be broken."

Still another said, "It's fortunate that we don't have to keep them anymore."

One woman, however, paused and said quietly: "I think God loved us a lot to give them to us—to protect us from ourselves" (*The Concordia Pulpit for 1982*, 79).

There was wisdom in that last woman's words. God's Law indeed protects us. Some of the commandments are arranged in ever-widening circles of protection: the Fifth Commandment protects the persons of our neighbors; the Sixth protects those closest to our neighbors, their spouses; the Seventh protects their property and business; and the Eighth guards their good names. We mentioned earlier in this lesson that the Lord has arranged things in this world so that He provides particular blessings to those who walk in certain ways of obedience.

But the protective intent behind God's Law comes as cold comfort to those who realize the stubborn fact of God—that He is God and they are not—and who further realize that they have been foolishly trying to switch these roles. For example, the adulteress not only harms herself and her illicit partners; moreover, she ignores God's covenant (Proverbs 2:17). Time and again, the Law exposes our guilt before Him. The stubborn fact of an all-seeing God spells judgment and wrath for all who play the fool and live in unrighteousness.

Unquestionably, (28:26) "he who trusts in himself is a fool"; but, at the same time, "he who walks in wisdom is kept safe." Those who walk in wisdom are none other than those who trust in the Lord. (Compare Proverbs 29:25.) (15:33) "The fear of the LORD [that is, fear tempered by trust in His grace and mercy] teaches a man wisdom." As we saw in Proverbs 8, the Lord Jesus Christ Himself is Wisdom. His delight in human beings moved Him to come into this world, lay down His own life as payment for the sin of the world, and then take it up again.

The Book of Proverbs does not tell the whole Gospel story, but it does proclaim the Gospel. It informs the wise that, despite their sin, they have a bright future with the Lord God. (24:14) "Know also that wisdom is sweet to your soul; if you find it, there is a future hope for you, and your hope will not be cut off."

4 Proverbs and Its Proverbs

In your readings this week you came across a pair of proverbs that seemed to contradict themselves. These sayings were meant to be mulled over, not quickly set aside. The aim of a proverb is to involve one's whole self with its wisdom so that the proverb engages not only our thinking, but also our priorities, our character, and our relationship to God.

Our everyday proverbs are generally brief, pithy, and simple: "Practice makes perfect"; "out of sight, out of mind"; "too many cooks spoil the broth." But biblical "proverbs" tend to make their point differently, through comparison, contrast, or even "contradiction" (i.e., paradox). Of course, when so much is compressed into so few words, something can be left out. All proverbial expressions are partial generalizations. While "he who hesitates is lost," it's also good to "look before you leap." Knowing when to apply each saying requires wisdom. So also, these biblical proverbs are found right next to each other:

> (26:4–5) Do not answer a fool according to his folly, or you will be like him yourself.
>
> Answer a fool according to his folly, or he will be wise in his own eyes.

These, too, are partial generalizations. They do not spoon feed. They goad us into thought.

This point can help us read Proverbs. In some of its passages God seems to say certain things are going to happen, but we may not see them fulfilled as we expect. (13:9) "The light of the righteous shines brightly, but the lamp of the wicked is snuffed out," says Proverbs. But Job (21:17) asks how often the lamp of the wicked really is snuffed out in this life. The point is that Proverbs describes general outcomes of general principles. Wisdom speaks generally, as wise people recognize.

(Proverbs 1:5) "Let the wise listen and add to their learning, and let the discerning get guidance." They get "steering" that enables them to move through the world adroitly. For it is God's world.

Conclusion

At the beginning of this presentation we noted that gold is gold no matter who finds it. Truth is truth whether a Christian or a pagan discovers it. But for the good of the world, it does matter who holds the truth and who holds the gold. The wicked and unbelievers will use their gold and the truth for their wicked and faithless goals. For the good of all, God calls His people to serve in every honorable vocation with wisdom. (23:23) "Buy the truth and do not sell it; get wisdom, discipline and understanding." Whether you are married or single, whether you work at home or for the largest corporation, mingle holy wisdom with the truth you hold and administer it in your family and society. As Jesus stated in the Sermon on the Mount (Matthew 5:13–16), you are salt in a tasteless world. You are light in the midst of darkness.

Christ, the Light of the World, is your light and life. Through His Word He will shine upon you with inspiration and encouragement to face the challenges of this age. His Word is more precious than gold, stocks, or bonds. The truth of forgiveness through His precious blood is more precious than all other knowledge because it drives away all fear and rolls away all doubt. As the wise say:

> (23:17–18) Do not let your heart envy sinners, but always be zealous for the fear of the Lord. There is surely a future hope for you, and your hope will not be cut off.

Concluding Activities

Make any necessary announcements. Distribute study leaflet 8.

Wisdom for Hezekiah's Court

Proverbs 25–29

Preparing for the Session

Central Focus

"When the righteous thrive, the people rejoice; when the wicked rule, the people groan" (Proverbs 29:2).

Objectives

That participants, by the power of the Holy Spirit working through the Word, will

1. understand the court wisdom of this section of Proverbs;

2. be able to describe the general teaching of Proverbs on love for one's neighbor.

3. look to Christ as the power behind their love as well as the pattern for it.

Note for small-group leaders: Lesson notes and other materials you will need begin on page 61.

For the Lecture Leader

In this lesson, we continue to consider the second table of the law. (The two "tables" relate to the two summaries of the Ten Commandments—table 1, love for God [Matthew 22:37], and table 2, love of the neighbor [Matthew 22:39].)

Session Plan

Worship

Begin the session with the hymn and prayer printed in the study leaflet. Accompaniments are available in denominational hymnals, such as *Lutheran Service Book* (refer to hymnal index).

Lecture Presentation

Introduction

Failure to follow through often presents a problem for golfers. Putting or driving, a shot will tend to go off course if the golfer does not complete his or her swing. Our relationship with the Lord has a natural follow through as well: love for our neighbors. We are loved and saved by God through faith in Jesus Christ, apart from our works. But this faith needs to follow through; it is bound to produce fruit: works done in love.

Martin Luther wrote in 1520 that "A Christian lives not in himself, but in Christ and in his neighbor. He lives in Christ through faith, in his neighbor through love. By faith he is caught up beyond himself into God. By love he descends beneath himself into his neighbor. Yet he always remains in God and in His love" (LW 31:371). The love with which God fills the lives of Christians in effect "spills over" from us to others.

The Book of Proverbs provides us a good basis for a discussion of such love. At least roughly speaking, as one commentator has summarized, "In the Bible's wisdom literature, Job emphasizes *faith* amid life's trials; the Psalms are alive with *hope;* and Proverbs is the wisdom born of *love*" (Ehlke, 3). We will see in this lesson that Proverbs has a great deal to say about the love that the wise have for their neighbors.

The frequent appearance of certain terms and topics in this collection of proverbs helps us understand the use of the collection. Listen to the following list of terms from Proverbs 25–29 and consider whom these proverbs might serve: king, ruler, master, honey, gold, silver, throne, prince, the poor, and friend. It's not that these words don't occur in other parts of Proverbs. They simply occur more often in this collection made by the men of Hezekiah, king of Judah. It seems clear that this collection was specifically created to guide the leadership of Judah, the young men in Hezekiah's court who served the poorer members of the kingdom.

1   Love for the Neighbor

Early in the twentieth century, a sociology professor assigned his class to interview 200 boys in a city slum. He said, "Predict their future." The sociology students estimated some 90 percent of the 200 would eventually serve time in prison. Twenty-five years later, the same professor got another class to find as many of the 200 as possible and learn what had happened to them. Some 180 were located, but only four of them had ever been in jail! The professor and his students searched for some common factor that had made such a difference in the lives of these boys grown into men. It turned out that over 100 of them said they were tremendously influenced by a high school teacher named Miss O'Rourke. After some searching, the now 70-year-old Sheila O'Rourke was found and interviewed. Somewhat puzzled, she could only offer this explanation: "All I can say is that I loved every one of them" (*Sermon Illustrations for Gospel Lessons, Series B* [St. Louis: CPH, 1981], 18).

Like Miss O'Rourke, the Book of Proverbs approaches the subject of the wise and their neighbors with a decidedly individual focus. Our "neighbor" is someone who needs our love. (14:21) "He who despises his neighbor sins," Proverbs says, "but blessed is he who is kind to the needy."

The neighbor is to be loved. Love is selfless giving in a timely fashion. (3:28) "Do not say to your neighbor, 'Come back later; I'll give it tomorrow'—when you now have it with you." God Himself is loved in this love for the needy. (19:17) "He who is kind to the poor lends to the LORD." On the other hand, (17:5) "He who mocks the poor shows contempt for their Maker."

2   Riches and Poverty

The Book of Proverbs takes a very realistic view concerning money, or the lack thereof, and what it can mean for human relations. In an extreme situation, (13:8) "a man's riches may ransom his life." The Lord Himself is the great leveler between rich and poor. (22:2) "Rich and poor have this in common: The LORD is the Maker of them all" (see 29:13).

When Cortez came to what is now Mexico, he told the natives, "The white man has a big sickness in his heart that can be eased only with gold" (Eldon Weisheit, *Let's Illustrate* [St. Louis: CPH, 1998], 234). By contrast, Proverbs declares that dishonest money—a fortune made by lying—not only slips through the fingers of people but also becomes a snare for them (see 13:11 and 21:6). The Book prefers (19:1) "a poor man whose walk is blameless" to a "fool whose lips are perverse."

In Proverbs, hoarding is frowned upon not only by people in general but also by God. (11:24) "One man gives freely, yet gains even more; another withholds unduly, but comes to poverty." (See also vv. 25–26.) God blesses the generous who share their food with the poor. Further, those who have money should also speak up for the poor (31:8–9) just as the Lord Himself takes up their cause. (See also 22:22–23.)

Ultimately, money is a matter between a person and God. The Book of Proverbs told the Israelites and it still tells us: (3:9–10) "Honor the LORD with your wealth, with the firstfruits of all your crops; then your barns will be filled to overflowing, and your vats will brim over with new wine." Again, caution is necessary in reading verses like these. Proverbs is not saying that wisdom is the sure-fire way to riches or that all the rich got that way by being wise. It mentions, for example, (28:11) "a rich man [who] may be wise in his own eyes," but only in his own eyes. The verse continues, "a poor man who has discernment sees through him."

3   Contentment

Over a number of years, a farmer had gotten increasingly fed up with his farm. He kept voicing his discontents to his friends, complaining about everything. He was making his friends miserable with his litany of complaints. His best friend hardly wanted to speak with him.

Finally, the farmer decided to sell. He scratched out an ad to place in the newspaper. Before submitting it, he wanted to try it out on someone. He cornered his best friend and read the ad to him: excellent location . . . fine equipment . . . fertile land . . . well-bred stock. "Wait a second," the farmer interrupted himself. "I'm changing my mind. All my life I've been looking for a place like that. I'm not gonna sell." You should have seen the look on his friend's face (adapted from Deffner, *Seasonal Illustrations for Preaching and Teaching*, 80).

Contentment, or a lack of contentment, can no more be kept "between one's ears" than an attitude toward money. (17:1) "Better a dry crust with peace and quiet than a house full of feasting, with strife." It also affects the bodily health of the discontented person: (14:30) "A heart at peace gives life to the body, but envy rots the bones."

Proverbs lists five things that surpass wealth in importance. It advises someone who wants to be wise to find contentment, if necessary, in them.

1. (15:16) Better a little with the *fear of the Lord* than great wealth with turmoil."

2. (16:8) "Better a little *with righteousness* than much gain with injustice."

3. (16:9) "Better to be *lowly in spirit* and among the oppressed than to share plunder with the proud."

4. (22:1) "A *good name* is more desirable than great riches."

5. (28:6) "Better a poor man whose *walk is blameless* than a rich man whose ways are perverse."

Most of the preferred items in these passages, it should be noted, are components in a relationship with God. Others are components in one's relationship with neighbors. They are more valuable than money.

In short, Proverbs counsels a contented attitude like that of the psalmist who said to the Lord in prayer: (Psalm 73:25–26) "Whom have I in heaven but You? And earth has nothing I desire besides You. My flesh and my heart may fail, but God is the strength of my heart and my portion forever." People with such an attitude are in a position to be helpful to others.

4 Friends and Enemies

(17:17) "A friend loves at all times," says the Book of Proverbs, but (18:1) "an unfriendly man pursues selfish ends." While the book recognizes what we call "the fair-weather friend," it reserves some of its most positive words for genuine friendship. (18:24) "A man of many companions may come to ruin, but there is a friend who sticks closer than a brother." (27:9b) "The pleasantness of one's friend springs from his earnest counsel." (27:6) Even "wounds from a friend can be trusted, but an enemy multiplies kisses."

Proverbs has several words of wisdom on friendship and being a friend:

1. Choose your friends wisely. (13:20) "He who walks with the wise grows wise, but a companion of fools suffers harm" (see also 12:26).

2. (3:29) "Do not plot harm against your neighbor, who lives trustfully near you."

3. Do not try to gain friends through flattery. (29:5) "Whoever flatters his neighbor is spreading a net for his feet."

4. Practice an apt sense of timing borne of wisdom. (27:14) "If a man loudly blesses his neighbor early in the morning, it will be taken as a curse."

5. Avoid overfamiliarity: (25:17) "Seldom set foot in your neighbor's house—too much of you, and he will hate you."

6. Do not speak of a friend's sins: (17:9) "He who covers over an offense promotes love, but whoever repeats the matter separates close friends."

7. And last, but never least, (27:10) "Do not forsake your friend."

Love is not only for friends. It is also to be extended to enemies. While Abraham Lincoln's political popularity was growing throughout the United States during the mid-1800s, he was not liked by everybody. For one, Edwin Stanton treated Lincoln with contempt, calling him a "low cunning clown" and "the original gorilla." Lincoln made no reply. In fact, when Lincoln was elected president, he appointed Stanton to be Secretary of War. He thought there was no one better to do the job. Lincoln treated Stanton with every courtesy. Four years later, Stanton was with the president on the night of the assassination. In the small room where Lincoln was taken after the shooting, Stanton said through his tears: "There lies the greatest leader of men the world has ever seen" (Green, 258–59). Lincoln had done the sort of thing Proverbs is talking about when it says, (25:21–22) "If your enemy is hungry, give him food to eat; if he is thirsty, give him water to drink. In doing this, you will heap burning coals on his head, and the Lord will reward you." In the New Testament, Paul quotes these words to urge overcoming evil with good (Romans 12:20). "Burning coals" are painful, but hopefully they prompt repentance so that the enemy becomes a friend.

5 Our Forgiveness and God's

A Christian psychologist was answering questions posed by a group of college students. One wanted him to identify the foremost cause of fatigue.

The doctor threw the question back to the group. "What do you think?" he said.

"Worry," was the first guess.

Someone else said, "Conflict."

"Wrong," the doctor replied. "It is unresolved guilt and unforgiven sin" (Arnold and Fry, 74).

(Proverbs 10:12) "Hatred stirs up dissension," says Proverbs, "but love covers over all wrongs." This refers to the realm of personal relationships, overlooking and forgiving our neighbor's sins. When Proverbs elsewhere says that (16:6) "Through love and faithfulness sin is atoned for," it is not referring to atoning for sin before God, but instead once again it is talking about one's relationships with other people. As the next verse continues, (16:7) "When a man's ways are pleasing to the Lord, he makes even his enemies live at peace with him."

Still more than peace with their neighbors, however, people need the forgiveness that God alone gives on account of the Messiah. Already in the Old Testament they could hear about it from the lips of God's people. (11:30) "The fruit of the righteous is a tree of life, and he who wins souls is wise." This is the most overtly "evangelistic" verse in Proverbs. It resembles Daniel's words: (Daniel 12:3) "Those who are wise will shine like the brightness of the heavens, and those who lead many to righteousness, like the stars for ever and ever." A similar evangelistic verse in Proverbs is comparable: (13:14) "The teaching of the wise is a fountain of life, turning a man from the snares of death." Extending God's forgiveness to people through telling them the Good News about Jesus is the greatest service of love we can perform for them. It is the wise thing to do.

Conclusion

You and I may not think we have much to give our neighbors. But in Christ we always have something to give them. We give ourselves because Christ gave Himself for us. (John 15:3) "Greater love has no one

than this," said Jesus, "that he lay down his life for his friends."

Concluding Activities

Make any necessary announcements. Distribute study leaflet 9.

Words from Agur, Lemuel, and a Happy Household

Proverbs 30–31

Preparing for the Session

Central Focus

Love for the neighbor, which results from God's love for us, manifests itself first at home. Based on Proverbs and other biblical books, this lesson focuses on the home life of the wise.

Objectives

That participants, by the power of the Holy Spirit working through the Word, will

1. be able to trace basic biblical connections between home relationships and the Gospel;

2. be able to describe the teaching of Proverbs about the wise and their home life;

3. want to live in accord with wisdom at home.

Note for small-group leaders: Lesson notes and other materials you will need begin on page 63.

For the Lecture Leader

The second table of the law, on love for the neighbor, prominently includes two commandments specifically treating relationships in the home: the Fourth and Sixth. The present lesson is directed specifically to home and family relationships.

Session Plan

Worship

Begin the session with the hymn and prayer printed in the study leaflet. Accompaniments are available in denominational hymnals, such as *Lutheran Service Book* (refer to hymnal index).

Lecture Presentation

Introduction

There are interesting Gospel connections to everything said about marriage and the family in the Bible, including in the Book of Proverbs. Scripture itself calls attention to these connections.

When Paul wrote to the Ephesians about marriage, he likened the relationship of husband and wife to that of Christ and the church: (Ephesians 5:23–27) "the husband is the head of the wife as Christ is the head of the church, His body. . . . Christ loved the church and gave Himself up for her to make her holy, cleansing her by the washing with water through the word, and to present her to Himself as a radiant church, without stain or wrinkle or any other blemish, but holy and blameless." Paul went on to quote Genesis, (Ephesians 5:31) "'For this reason a man will leave his father and mother and be united to his wife, and the two will become one flesh'." Then he added, (v. 32) "This is a profound mystery—but I am talking about Christ and the church." Marriage reflects the relationship between Christ and the church. Therefore, while marriage is a worthwhile topic in and of itself, it claims the attention and the effort of Christ's wise disciples all the more because of this Gospel connection.

Likewise, Paul wrote the Galatians: (3:26) "You are all sons of God through faith in Christ Jesus." Sons are not slaves; they are heirs (see Galatians 4:7). We are co-heirs with Christ (Romans 8:17). Because He is our Brother and made us His brothers and sisters through faith, God is our Father—despite our sin and guilt.

We do not comprehend the full significance of these connections between the Gospel and the marriage relationship and between the Gospel and the relationship of a father or mother to children. As the apostle pointed out, there is mystery here. But it is with minds fixed on the Gospel that we turn our eyes toward Proverbs and its teachings on the wise at home.

1 Marriage

The Lord God intended marriage for the good of people, not their ill. He made Eve as a suitable helper for Adam. At first sight, Adam realized the blessing God had given him through Eve: (Genesis 2:23) "This is now bone of my bones and flesh of my flesh; she shall be called 'woman,' for she was taken out of man" (see Genesis 2:18–25). Despite the fall into sin, God continues to grant blessings through marriage. (Proverbs 18:22) "He who finds a wife finds what is good and receives favor from the LORD," says the Book of Proverbs.

Of course, the good blessings of marriage and the family life established within it can turn sour due to sin and folly. Proverbs says that (19:13) "A foolish son is his father's ruin, and a quarrelsome wife is like a constant dripping." In such circumstances people really don't live happily; they have simply gotten married and had children. Wisdom is needed in the home, and Proverbs has much wisdom to offer for this sphere of life.

The initial chapters of the Book contain an expression of appreciation for marriage, including its physical dimension. Instead of falling into the traps of the adulteress, the young man is advised to (5:15–17) "Drink water from your own cistern, running water from your own well. . . . Let them be yours alone, never to be shared with strangers." In case there is any doubt as to the meaning of this figurative language, the next verse says, (5:18b) "may you rejoice in the wife of your youth." Then the next verse adds, together with touches of frank detail, (5:19c) "may you ever be captivated by her love."

Because marriage consists in so much more than sex, it is terrible to be married and unloved (Proverbs 30:21, 23). The marriage relationship is total, involving every aspect of one's being. This point is brought home in Proverbs through a number of thought-provoking references to women.

2 A Godly Wife

Most of the proverbs in the Book are addressed to male hearers, "my son" or "my sons." But if Proverbs apparently sees through the eyes of a man, as it were, it nonetheless has much to say about mankind in the female gender: (Proverbs 19:14) "Houses and wealth are inherited from parents, but a prudent wife is from the LORD."

It is important to realize that not all women are so virtuous. Early in the book, folly is compared to a loud, undisciplined woman (9:13). Later, Proverbs insists that living either in a corner of the roof or out in the desert is more pleasant than living with a quarrelsome wife (21:9, 19). Elsewhere, it likens a quarrelsome wife to (27:15–16) "constant dripping on a rainy day; restraining her," it continues, "is like restraining the wind or grasping oil with the hand." Even more graphically, (11:22) "Like a gold ring in a pig's snout is a beautiful woman who shows no discretion."

While (12:4) "a disgraceful wife is like decay in his [her husband's] bones," it is also true that "a wife of noble character is her husband's crown." Similarly, (14:1) "The wise woman builds her house, but with her own hands the foolish one tears hers down." Proverbs affirms that (11:16) "a kindhearted woman gains respect."

Above all, it is not physical attractiveness but moral qualities that mark the ideal woman described throughout the Book of Proverbs, and especially in its last 22 verses. These verses were written in Hebrew as an alphabetic poem. The first line began with the first letter of the Hebrew alphabet, and each successive line started with the next letter. The wife of noble character is valuable (31:10). She is trustworthy (v. 11), good to her husband (v. 12), industrious, (vv. 13–15, 18–19, 21–24), strong in work and sharp of mind (vv. 16–18, 27). The woman depicted here is from a family of means, and she is involved in business. But her concerns "clearly center around her home and family" (Ehlke, 315). Further, she is generous (v. 20), dignified and hopeful (v. 25), and, of course, wise (v. 26). (V. 28) "Her children arise and call her blessed; her husband also." In short, (v. 30) "Charm is deceptive, and beauty is fleeting; but a woman who fears the LORD is to be praised." The wife of Proverbs 31 gives us powerful positive examples of the many dimensions of marriage.

3 Parents and Their Children

To be ready for their future responsibilities, children need discipline in the present. Both parents providing discipline and children receiving it should remember that (3:12) "the LORD disciplines those He loves, as a father the son he delights in." In fact, parents act as

God's representatives as they discipline their children.

Discipline is necessary because folly always lies so close at hand. In a twist on the term "original sin," we might say that Proverbs teaches "original folly." It says, (22:15) "Folly is bound up in the heart of a child, but the rod of discipline will drive it far from him." That is, (29:15) "The rod of correction imparts wisdom." This verse goes on to say that "a child left to himself disgraces his mother." Children dare not be left to themselves. They need discipline (here called "the rod").

(Hebrews 12:11) "No discipline seems pleasant at the time, but painful," says the Book of Hebrews. But parents are to discipline their children as an aspect of loving them. (Proverbs 13:24) "He who spares the rod hates his son, but he who loves him is careful to discipline him." A little pain now can save a child from ruin later: (23:13–14) "Do not withhold discipline from a child; if you punish him with the rod, he will not die. Punish him with the rod and save his soul from death." Discipline is a forward-looking act, an act of hope. (See Proverbs 19:18.)

In addition to discipline through punishment, parents also teach their children by example. A little girl was painstakingly following her father's steps through a new garden. She told him, "Daddy, if you don't get mud on *your* feet, I won't get any mud on me" (Green, 147). Proverbs says, (20:7) "The righteous man leads a blameless life; blessed are his children after him."

Parents need to start early with discipline, for it takes time. (20:21) "An inheritance quickly gained at the beginning will not be blessed at the end" because the young heir does not have the discipline for it. But the considerable time and effort involved in instilling discipline in the young proves to be worth it. (29:17) "Discipline your son, and he will give you peace; he will bring delight to your soul." Similarly, (23:24) "the father of a righteous man has great joy; he who has a wise son delights in him." For (10:1) "a wise son brings joy to his father, but a foolish son grief to his mother" (see also Proverbs 17:21, 25). Proverbs pictures a parent saying, (23:15–16) "My son, if your heart is wise, then my heart will be glad; my inmost being will rejoice when your lips speak what is right."

4 Children and Their Parents

If parents bear the responsibility to teach and discipline their children, then the role of the children is to learn. (13:1) "A wise son heeds his father's instruction, but a mocker does not listen to rebuke." It is a fool who (15:5) "spurns his father's discipline." For (20:11) "even a child is known by his actions, by whether his conduct is pure and right."

Proverbs warns, in frightful imagery: (30:17) "The eye that mocks a father, that scorns obedience to a mother, will be pecked out by the ravens of the valley, will be eaten by the vultures." As noted in a previous lesson, King Solomon began his reign wisely and well. But he ended it foolishly and under God's judgment. (Contrast 1 Kings 3 with 1 Kings 11.) His son Rehoboam, born about the time when Solomon started to reign, had as a boy no doubt heard both Solomon's own wisdom and his admonitions to seek wisdom. (Solomon reigned over all Israel for 40 years; 1 Kings 11:42.) Rehoboam was 41 years old when he became king (1 Kings 14:21). As the heir apparent, he probably heard godly admonitions repeatedly. Yet soon after he became king, Rehoboam discounted what his father said: (Proverbs 4:6) "Do not forsake wisdom, and she will protect you." Specifically, Rehoboam ignored the advice of his older and wiser counselors to lighten the load of labor on Israel's northern tribes. Instead, he made it heavier yet (1 Kings 12:1–11). Then the northern tribes rebelled. Rehoboam ended up losing much more than his eye; he lost most of the kingdom (vv. 16–19).

So what about the proverb that says, (22:6) "Train a child in the way he should go, and when he is old he will not turn from it"? What about David's training of Solomon or Solomon's of Rehoboam? As stated earlier, this proverb makes a general statement. There can be exceptions. But the statement is still most apt. A commentator puts it this way: "One's childhood training in the Bible is never entirely forgotten. It's always there as a reminder, a corrective, and a directive on the path to heaven" (Ehlke, 213). The Bible does not comment directly on the condition of Solomon's heart at the end of his days, but the indications are not encouraging. However, there are these hopeful words on Rehoboam: (2 Chronicles 12:12) "Because Rehoboam humbled himself, the Lord's anger turned from him, and he was not totally destroyed. Indeed, there was some good in Judah." When Rehoboam was old, he remembered.

The overall attitude of children toward their parents should be to bless them, not curse them. (Proverbs 20:20) "If a man curses his father or mother, his lamp will be snuffed out in pitch darkness" Proverbs warns. Elsewhere, Proverbs says, (17:6b) "Parents are the pride of their children."

(20:29) Strength belongs to the young, experience and wisdom to the old. Grown children, who have both strength and wisdom, bear responsibilities toward their elderly parents: (23:22b) "Do not despise your mother when she is old."

It should be noted, finally, that the Lord Himself takes particular interest in fatherless children. (23:10–11) "Do not . . . encroach on the fields of the fatherless, for their Defender is strong; he will take up their case against you." The word translated "Defender" is a "Redeemer," as in the Book of Ruth (Ruth 2:20) or in the triumphant shout of Job, (19:25) "I know that my Redeemer lives." A redeemer is a brother or other close relative who is responsible for someone who cannot act in his or her own behalf. A redeemer helps others out of trouble, buys them back from bondage, and, if necessary, becomes their substitute. No one plays this role better than God Himself. He played it for the whole world in Christ.

Conclusion

A new pastor came to visit a family at home. While he was there, getting to know this family, he raised a question. He did not ask how often they were in the habit of going to church. He did not ask how much the family contributed to the congregation. He didn't want to know about their standing in the community or the number of groups they were all involved in. On that day, all he asked was, "Does Christ live here?" (Merkens, 63).

Christ is where His people are. Apply His wisdom from Proverbs in your home. His people are where His Word is. In a home where people hear about their sin and His forgiveness, Jesus lives. When He lives in a home, He imparts wisdom.

Concluding Activities

Make any necessary announcements. (You may want to announce the next LifeLight course. If it is to begin soon, you may want to distribute study leaflets for the course to all those whom have committed themselves to participate.)

Close with prayer something like this: Thank You, Lord Jesus, for the opportunity to study—and to grow—through Your Word. Thanks, too, for the fellowship of Your saints as we have shared Your Word with one another. Keep us in Your Word always. Amen.

Small-Group Leaders Material

The Beginning of Wisdom

1 Kings 3–7; Proverbs 1:1–7

Preparing for the Session

Central Focus

"The fear of the Lord is the beginning of wisdom" (Proverbs 9:10). This study of Proverbs starts by examining "wisdom," and "the fear of the Lord" in light of the book's initial admonitions to avoid foolishness and seek wisdom.

Objectives

That participants, by the power of the Holy Spirit working through the Word, will

1. be able to describe several facets of the biblical concept of wisdom;

2. appreciate strengths and limitations of the proverb as a form for communicating truth;

3. be able to differentiate the "fear of the Lord" from slavelike fear on biblical grounds and recognize its importance both in the Book of Proverbs and in their lives;

4. want to be wise in accord with the appeals in Proverbs 1.

Small-Group Discussion Helps

Day 1 • 1 Kings 3

1. (a) Ultimately, Solomon was wise because the Lord gave him wisdom. The king in no way deserved it. (b) His prayer for wisdom came at a time when he was habitually offering sacrifices on the "high places," probably former Canaanite sacrificial sites (v. 3). In Near Eastern religious thought, higher elevations were closer to heaven and, therefore, ideal places for communicating with the gods. The Israelites were supposed to make their offerings at one location: the tabernacle (see Deuteronomy 12:2–5). Despite Solomon's inconsistency regarding proper worship, the Lord nonetheless invited Solomon to ask for whatever he wanted (v. 5).

2. (a) Solomon was to govern God's people. He wanted to do this well, not only in service to others but also in worship of God. His request showed humility, an ability to assess circumstances realistically, a sense of responsibility, a sense of dependence upon God, and confidence that the Lord would help. He already had a measure of the "fear of the Lord" (see Proverbs 1:7), which turns out to be a recurrent theme in Proverbs. (b) Answers will vary on how we can emulate Solomon's example. This course on Proverbs should provide us a heightened wisdom and a deeper relationship with God.

3. Solomon took stock of a complex situation, came to grips with evil, and corrected the wrong in a fair and compassionate way. His decision was an effective practical step toward helping all concerned—the two women and the baby—to live in harmony with God in the order of creation.

Day 2 • Read 1 Kings 4:20–6:38

4. Solomon had *administrative wisdom*, which included finding the best talent and delegating responsibility wisely (1 Kings 4:1, 21; 5:6; 7:13–14); *intellectual wisdom* (1 Kings 4:29–34; 10:1–9); and *spiritual wisdom*, including an "evangelistic" concern (1 Kings 8:27–30, 41–43).

5. The people of Israel had grown as numerous as "the sand on the seashore" and possessed the Promised Land.

6. Israel had rest from its enemies and completely possessed the land. As David's descendant, Solomon extended his reign and continued the lineage from which the Messiah would be born and would establish an eternal kingdom.

Day 3 • Read 1 Kings 7:1–12 and Psalm 72:1–7

7. Solomon completed his palace, a colonnade, the Hall of Justice, and a palace for Pharaoh's daughter.

8. Solomon spent almost twice the amount of time building his palace (13 years) as he did to build the temple (7 years). Solomon became more and more self-centered as time went on.

9. Answers will vary. Like Jesus, Solomon had God's righteousness, he judged fairly, he defended the afflicted, genuine worship prospered under his leadership, he ruled broadly, kings bowed down to him, he showed compassion, he had a glorious name, and all nations were blessed through him.

Day 4 • Read Proverbs 1:1–7

10. (a) Examples will vary, but might include "practice makes perfect"; "out of sight, out of mind"; or "too many cooks spoil the broth." (b) In general, secular proverbs encapsulate collective past experiences in brief and striking ways in order to illuminate present situations. Often (as with "too many cooks spoil the broth") the proverb's message has application far beyond the setting literally mentioned in the wording. Proverbs advise people to adjust themselves to the way things are in the created world or in society. Someone who doesn't "get it" is foolish.

11. Since wisdom is more than mere knowledge, a proverb in the mouth of a fool is not merely misunderstood; it is useless and potentially harmful. The Book of Proverbs aims to engage not only our thinking, but also our priorities, our character, and our relationship with God. The question is less-than-elegantly worded in order to call attention to the word *for*, which begins verses 2a, 2b, 3, and 4 in the NIV. Proverbs are for attaining (grasping, almost "experiencing") wisdom; understanding deep thoughts; acquiring the discipline of wise behavior, that is, righteousness, justice, and equity; giving good sense to those who are inexperienced and lack judgment.

These purposes are, it should be noted, both cognitive and affective. They are even partly vocational, preparing people for work and leadership.

12. Everyone needs it. The young are inexperienced and need to grow in maturity. Those who are already wise and discerning need to increase their capacity to receive wisdom so they can continue moving adroitly through God's world. Proverbs, parables, and the sayings and riddles of the wise are not to be considered once and then cast aside. They become a lifelong study.

13. "The fear of the LORD" is compared negatively with hating knowledge; being wise in one's own eyes; pride, arrogance, evil behavior, and perverse speech; being devious in one's ways; envying sinners; and hardening one's heart.

Day 5 • Proverbs 1:7

14. The "fear of the LORD" is linked with walking in uprightness, instruction in wisdom, and avoidance of evil. To "fear the LORD" is to believe and practice the faith revealed in the Old Testament.

15. The "fear of the LORD" in Proverbs 1:7 is a childlike fear. Sinners can only have this kind of fear of God when they have received His forgiveness on account of Christ by faith. God's Old Testament people—the people who first heard the proverbs in the Book of Proverbs—knew about the coming Christ through Messianic prophecy.

16. Proverbs is divided into collections:

The Appeals of Wisdom (1–9)

The Proverbs of Solomon (10:1–22:16)

The Sayings of the Wise (22:17–24:34)

The Proverbs of Solomon copied by the men of Hezekiah (25–29)

The Sayings of Agur (30)

The Sayings of King Lemuel and a poem about a wife of noble character (31)

The arrangement of Proverbs 10–31, which mixes together proverbs on various subjects, can help us apply the proverbial material to life as it is. For example, we typically do not think exclusively about money one day, family concerns the next day, work the next, and our relationship with God the next. Instead, a number of concerns confront us simultaneously every day. (Participants may wish to reflect further on the miscellaneous and unpredictable character of life.) Our challenge is to engage these various concerns wisely, out of a personal center integrated around the fear of the Lord.

The Way of Life and the Way of Death—Part 1

Proverbs 1:8–3:35

Preparing for the Session

Central Focus

"Trust in the LORD with all your heart and lean not on your own understanding; in all your ways acknowledge Him, and He will make your paths straight" (Proverbs 3:5–6).

Objectives

That participants, by the power of the Holy Spirit working through the Word, will

1. be able to contrast the way of wisdom with the way of folly as to their characteristics and their outcomes;

2. value the way of wisdom and want to avoid the way of folly.

Small-Group Discussion Helps

Day 1 • Deuteronomy 6

1. Education took place chiefly in the home and was led by the parents.

2. Deuteronomy describes an educational process based on memorization, learning things through repetition. The word translated "impress" also describes the process of sharpening, drawing a tool repeatedly over a whetstone.

3. The goal of instruction was to instill "the fear of the LORD."

4. Solomon and others may have collected proverbs to serve as education texts for specific ages or vocations.

Day 2 • Proverbs 1:8–33

5. Wisdom is learned from parents and wise teachers. "Sinners" attempt to entice one away from wisdom,

which shows once more that wisdom is much more than knowledge. The fear of the Lord is the beginning of wisdom.

6. Answers will vary. A key point is that greed and lust prevent people from seeing that they are harming themselves when they act. The Law as a curb in our sinful lives sometimes keeps us from overt sin, not because we love God and His right way as we should but because we fear the consequences of doing the wrong. At times, blinded by greed or some similar affection, we "jump the curb," acting foolishly and wrongly. In the fear of the Lord, we need to repent.

7. Three groups are addressed: simple ones, mockers, and fools. Simple ones merely love their simplicity, but fools hate knowledge. Mockers are still worse. In their pride and self-centeredness, they *delight* in their highly vocal mockery.

8. Wisdom offers not only *illumination* (1:22–24) and *advice* (1:25, 30) through the Word, but also *safety and security* (1:33). "Wisdom" here may be compared with the work of the Holy Spirit, who calls us by the Gospel, enlightens us with His gifts, sanctifies us, and keeps us in the true faith.

9. (a) Wisdom ridicules those who refuse to listen (1:26). Such people end up seeking, but not being able to find, wisdom (1:28; see Hosea 4:6; 5:6; Amos 8:11). Therefore, they eat the fruit of their own ways: death (1:31–32). (b) This disaster will be averted if people listen to wisdom.

Day 3 • Proverbs 2:1–22

10. The benefits mentioned are understanding the fear of the Lord, understanding what is right and just, rescue from the way of the wicked, rescue from the adulteress, and walking in the ways of the good. These are not intellectual benefits, but are moral and spiritual in nature.

11. Answers will vary. One characteristic that comes through with particular vividness in Proverbs 2 is the wise person's intimacy with God (vv. 5, 10).

12. (a) Advice: take God's Word to heart (Proverbs 2:1–2; compare 30:5–6) and earnestly pray (Proverbs 2:3) and meditate (see Proverbs 2:4). (It might be observed that the four respective phrases in vv. 3–4 build in intensity.) But recall, no matter how much you get involved with the diligent pursuit of wisdom, it is never innate within us or deserved by us. (b) Wisdom remains God's gift (Proverbs 2:6).

. . . .

Day 4 • Proverbs 3:1–12

13. Verses 3 and 4 are about loyalty to a loyal God; verses 5–6 deal with reliance upon the Lord; verses 7–8 tell us to avoid pride and evil, for our own good; verses 9–10 are about participation in sacrificial worship (firstfruits); and verses 11–12 are on acceptance of both God's instruction and His correction in suffering, for He is *the* true Teacher. In discussion, you might want to touch briefly on the application of each within the life of a Christian.

. . . .

Day 5 • Proverbs 3:13–35

14. (a) Wisdom brings profit greater than precious metal. Therefore, wisdom is more precious than jewels or anything else imaginable. (b) Wisdom brings long life, riches and honor, pleasant ways, and peace. Wisdom, this section goes on to say, is the source of life ("tree of life," v. 18). (Verses 18–20 snap into sharper focus in light of the identification of God the Son as Wisdom in chapter 8, as will be noted in Lesson 4 of this course.)

15. In those who fear the Lord, heed His Word, and learn the lessons of wisdom, there develops a sort of shrewdness that enables success in life (albeit not according to the world's standards; see Proverbs 4:11–12, 14). They acquire the skill to function well in the world that God made. This sort of success generally involves safety, freedom from fear, and confidence in the Lord. And come what may in this world, when the Lord is on our side, what can anyone else do to us?

16. (a) The prohibitions are against withholding good (v. 27) or even delaying it (v. 28); plotting harm against neighbors (v. 29); making false accusations (v. 30); and envying or emulating the violent (v. 31). (b) One who fears the Lord and has the blessings of wisdom does not need to seek security, reputation, or riches through any of these things. (c) Such persons enjoy intimacy with God.

17. Fools are "wicked" and "mockers." The Lord curses and mocks them, holding them up to shame. The wise are also righteous and humble. From the Lord they receive blessing, grace, and honor.

The Way of Life and the Way of Death—Part 2

Proverbs 4:1–8:21

Preparing for the Session

Central Focus

"Listen, my son, accept what I say, and the years of your life will be many. I guide you in the way of wisdom and lead you along straight paths" (Proverbs 4:10–11). God is most important in the lives of wise people. This lesson focuses upon the relationship of the wise with the just and gracious Lord, who speaks both judgment and mercy in the Book of Proverbs.

Objectives

That participants, by the power of the Holy Spirit working through the Word, will

1. identify the appeals from wisdom;

2. learn to avoid common temptations and pitfalls;

3. receive assurance of God's forgiveness for past and present failures.

Small-Group Discussion Helps

Day 1• Proverbs 4

1. Wisdom is not merely to be learned, but loved (v. 6). Further, wisdom watches over (v. 6), and exalts and honors (vv. 8–9) the one who embraces her.

2. Answers will vary. Wisdom entails long life, capable living in a way that is both right and safe, and the promise of a still-brighter future. Folly means obsession with evil and ultimately stumbling but not knowing precisely why.

3. Answers will vary. As much as possible, keep the discussion close to the text.

Day 2 • Proverbs 5

4. Solomon's greatest weakness was for sexual sin. He virtually collected wives and concubines. The repeated references to adultery in Proverbs show Solomon sincerely reflecting on his personal failures. Illicit sex forms a potent temptation, now as then. But the Old Testament also depicted apostasy and idolatry as adultery (Hosea 1–3). In such "spiritual adultery," proper affection for the true God is lost. Further, in the Canaanite religion surrounding Israel, cultic prostitution was a staple element. Overt sexual sin was bound up with idolatry.

5. Adultery destroys marriages and families. The pursuit of one-night stands can prevent a person from ever having a family. How ironic that the act of joining bodies should cause so much division! Jealousy and lust frequently lead to murder.

6. (a) They should acknowledge the truth of God's Word (confess), heed its teaching (repent), and return to the way of righteousness (renewal). (b) The path of life is paved with God's wise plan of salvation through Jesus' death and resurrection, unlike the path of the world, whose wisdom is foolish.

7. *For personal reflection. Sharing optional.* Answers will vary. Allow discreet discussion.

Day 3 • Proverbs 6

8. In general, it is the making of foolish financial commitments. The specific example given in the text is to take responsibility for the debts of strangers. A naive would-be helper can get caught in a crooked business deal. At the very least, such a person sets the stranger in a position of control over his or her life. Getting out of such a snare is worth humbling oneself and pleading with one's neighbor.

9. The second trap for the young is laziness.

10. Here and elsewhere Proverbs extols industry, like the ant's. This is remarkable since in the ancient Near East, people generally did not work unless they had to. They tended to think that work was beneath them. You might want to trace any similarities between this attitude and that of our society today.

11. In his relationship to his neighbors the scoundrel can do much more damage than one who is simply inexperienced and gullible. The scoundrel destroys the basis for community life. Before God, such people have grown more hardened than those who are simply naive. They revel in their sin and foolishness and have grown comfortable in it.

12. Solomon urges his son to bind God's Word around his neck and over the heart, the very locations such a necklace would be placed. God's Word was to serve as a light and guide, just as the blessing in Numbers calls for God's face to "shine" on the one receiving the blessing and calls on God to "keep" them.

. . . .

Day 4 • Proverbs 7

13. He put himself in the wrong place at the wrong time.

14. Her dress, her demeanor, and her behavior (the immediate kiss) are all brash. She even has the audacity to make a religious reference (v. 14) before extending a very frank and detailed invitation to fornication.

15. As throughout these early chapters, Proverbs repeatedly encourages engagement with wisdom and the sayings of the wise. As noted in session 1, the fear of the Lord forms the beginning of wisdom. This is a fear mixed with forgiveness and comfort in God's mercy. By God's mercies we can be transformed in renewal, not conformed to the world. It also helps to recall one's Baptism.

16. (a) God graciously forgave him. (b) Jesus extended the same gracious forgiveness to the woman. (c) The Lord is no less gracious to those who repent of such sins today. If you have failed to live a sexually pure and decent life in thought and deed, cast yourself upon God's care! Sincerely repent. He will forgive and comfort you.

. . . .

Day 5 • Proverbs 8:1–21

17. (a) Wisdom's invitation is extended out in the open, loudly and in a conspicuous place. (b) Wisdom doesn't hide itself, but rather makes itself known in the arena that we call daily life. Wisdom's public approach also makes for a striking contrast with that of the lurking adulterous woman in chapter 7.

18. Wisdom (a) calls out (b) to those in need, (c) giving true and worthy instruction (d) that is of incomparable value.

19. (a) Pride prevents the wicked from knowing God. (b) These sins especially provoke God's judgment. (c) Pride leads to self-righteousness.

20. (a) It is always true that the government of kings and princes—the governing authorities—is instituted by God. This forms another indication that "Wisdom" in chapter 8 is more than a quality or characteristic. (b) Believers are not simply to obey government but should diligently request God's blessings for those in authority. (c) Believers should only disobey those in authority when leaders command or pressure them to disobey God.

No Christ, No Wisdom; Know Christ, Know Wisdom

Proverbs 8:22–9:18

Preparing for the Session

Central Focus

Proverbs 8 is about Christ, the Son of God, who with the Father and the Holy Spirit is God from all eternity—this same Christ is identified by Proverbs 8 as the One who became incarnate and lives with us today as our Savior and Lord.

Objectives

That participants, by the power of the Holy Spirit working through the Word, will

1. be able to explain the identification of Jesus as Wisdom in Proverbs 8;

2. confide in Christ as Wisdom who gives wisdom and so much more;

3. be alert to relate Christ to the wise sayings in the rest of Proverbs.

4. be able to distinguish between three main ways of teaching wisdom in Proverbs;

5. desire to go the way of wisdom, not that of folly, in the fear of the Lord.

Small-Group Discussion Helps

Day 1 • Proverbs 8:22–31

1. The birth from eternity is the "eternal generation" of God the Son by God the Father. Jesus Christ is true God, begotten of the Father from eternity. As John 1 says, the "Word" of God—the Second Person of the Trinity—existed from all eternity and participated in the work of Creation. He Himself is the Wisdom of God. In Psalm 2:7 the Lord says to the Messiah (the Anointed One), "You are My Son; today I have become Your Father." This is another passage on the "eternal generation." Today and every day, the eternal Son

receives His being from the eternal Father. The well-known Christmas prophecy in Micah and Matthew affirms the incarnation and birth at Bethlehem of the eternal Son of God, the speaker in Proverbs 8:22–26. In His prayer in John 17 Jesus referred to His eternal relationship with God, a relationship about which we learn more via His words in Proverbs 8.

2. Not only was Wisdom with God at the creation of the world; He was a Master Workman, assisting in the work. For more on this point, see John 1:2–3 and Colossians 1:15–17.

3. (a) Not only did God the Son delight in God the Father's presence when the world was created, but He also rejoiced in the created world and delighted in mankind. (b) Scripture identifies Jesus with the Wisdom of God. Luke 11:49 says that the "Wisdom of God" (*not* "God in His wisdom," as the NIV translates) sent prophets and others to proclaim His message. Matthew 23:34 identifies Jesus Himself as the Sender.

4. Because Christ loved us, we respond with love for God and for our neighbors. We show this love by obeying the Lord.

Day 2 • Proverbs 8:32–36

5. (a) Listen to Wisdom and the instruction of Wisdom (vv. 32–33). Watch and wait at His door (v. 34), which is the opposite of hanging around the door to folly at the house of the adulteress (contrast Proverbs 5:8). (b) In our terms, this translates to going to church, reading and hearing God's Word, taking advantage of every opportunity to absorb His gracious teaching and live according to it. Notice that the premium here is on regularity, not novelty. (c) By wisdom we confess our faith, bear the message of the Gospel to others, and explain our faith to those who ask.

6. (a) The world regards God's wisdom in Christ as foolish and weak. (b) We listen to all that Wisdom teaches and wait upon the Lord as He teaches us more and leads us further in faith.

Day 3 • Proverbs 9:1–6

7. Today the house corresponds to the church. The church is built on Christ, and through her Christ offers people His Word. Through the church the invitation to wisdom goes out into all the world.

8. Answers will vary. They might include that the church, too, should be well prepared with the Gospel and Sacraments, extend her invitation prominently and vigorously, and be concerned not only to relieve ignorance but also to save lives.

9. Throughout Scripture the Lord uses the picture of a banquet to describe the joy, fellowship, and blessings He provides to the wise. They not only know about God's wisdom but also believe in it and act upon it. Likewise, Christ calls us not only to know of Him but also to act upon His promises, partaking of His blessings in the banquet of the Lord's Supper.

10. "Way" acknowledges that God deals with people in time and space throughout life. It accounts for the fact that God's involvement in human life is somewhat hidden (we don't know what He has in store for us "around the bend," as it were), but it emphasizes the firm and sure nature of His revelation (the way we are on). And "way" suggests that we are going somewhere. The destination for the wise is to see the Lord face-to-face.

Day 4 • Proverbs 9:7–9

11. Instruction is the most straightforward of the three ways of teaching. We should not be misled by this straightforwardness, however. Scorning instruction always carries a penalty. See Proverbs 13:13; 19:16.

12. Rebuke is more intense than instruction, but it can be quite salutary. It is appreciated by the wise, if not by fools.

13. Correction is frequently linked with "discipline." It implies that something has gone awry and straightening it out can prove painful.

Day 5 • Proverbs 9:10–18

14. In His holiness, the Lord finds detestable the following things: "a perverse man," "the thoughts of the wicked," "lying lips," deceptive business practices, "the proud of heart," rushing into evil, "hands that shed innocent blood," "a man who stirs up dissension among brothers," "the sacrifice of the wicked," "the way of the wicked," the prayers of those who turn deaf ears to the Law, and injustice.

15. God-fearing people are honored, yet humble. They are generous and faithful.

16. Wisdom has dignity, but folly does not. Folly still tries to imitate, though. From a prominent place, folly issues an invitation to the simple.

17. Answers will vary. Basic points include that the church has ungodly competition that is very enticing but misleading in the most profound way. Various forms of folly become the gateway to hell for countless people. In love for the neighbor, the church takes the saving Gospel into the world.

Wisdom Contrasts Good and Evil

Proverbs 10–15

Preparing for the Session

Central Focus

God's love for us results in our love not only for Him but also for our neighbor. This lesson takes a broad view of the teaching offered by Proverbs on the relationship between the wise and others.

Objectives

That participants, by the power of the Holy Spirit working through the Word, will

1. recognize significant themes in Proverbs;

2. be able to describe the relationship between the Lord and wise people;

3. be able to begin differentiating Law and Gospel in the Book of Proverbs;

4. be able to describe the teaching of Proverbs about the speech and attitudes of the wise;

5. want to conform themselves to wisdom in their attitudes and words;

6. grow in relationship to God and as a wise person.

Small-Group Discussion Helps

Day 1 • Proverbs 10

1. Through antithetic parallelism, apt contrasts can be drawn between the righteous and the wicked or between the way of the wise and the way of fools. Antithetic parallelism is especially common not only in Proverbs 10, but in chapters 11–15 as well.

2. Some of the antithetic proverbs in chapter 10 draw attention to actions and their consequences (e.g., vv. 4, 10, 19). But more antithetic proverbs in chapter 10—and certainly more in chapters 10–15—highlight character and the consequences it brings (e.g., vv. 2, 3, 6) or

the actions it entails (e.g., vv. 8, 12, 14). The main thing to concentrate on, then, is character. Proverbs says that character begins with one's relationship to God.

3. Taking care of our bodies out of thanks to Him who created these bodies results, on the whole, with the blessing of long life.

4. Even when the earthly life of the believer is cut short, eternal joy lies ahead. The wicked have nothing to look forward to after this brief life on earth. Their future is bleak and hopeless.

Day 2 • Proverbs 11

5. (a) Of ourselves, we are not—and cannot be made—righteous. (b) The text can only be referring to the righteousness that God gives us in Christ, which can only be received through faith in the Messiah.

6. As time permits, allow participants to share their answers. The desire of the wise is for God and the righteousness that He gives. In short, they seek "treasures in heaven." This is the ultimate good—and the opposite of wrath—no matter what else happens. Seeking righteousness in Christ through the Gospel and the Sacraments is a "no lose" proposition.

7. (a) The wise have been covered with the righteousness of Christ and are swept up into God's rescue mission for the world. They reach out to their neighbors with the saving Gospel. (b) Like Paul, we grow in our desire to share God's saving Gospel with all kinds and sorts of people because of the love of Christ and our own joy in the Gospel.

Day 3 • Proverbs 12

8. One who obtains the Lord's favor is one who has Christ, the Wisdom of God. Such a person finds life. From life in Christ flows the person's "goodness."

9. Caring for animals was a shrewd business move in a setting where they were critical to people economically (see Proverbs 27:23–24). But moreover—and this is the point here—kindness to animals manifests respect for God and His creation.

10. The righteousness of God in Christ, which is received by faith, delivers from death. To stay in that righteousness results in no eternal death. What a comfort!

Day 4 • Proverbs 13–14

11. Wisdom is productive. It brings forth wealth (both spiritual and physical) and, thereby, honor. Folly, by contrast, leads nowhere and yields only more folly.

12. Union with the living, exalted Christ is the secret of being content.

Day 5 • Proverbs 15

13. This news is only good for people who have the "fear of the Lord," which is the beginning of wisdom—that is, those whose fright is tempered by the forgiveness of sins on account of Christ and being covered with His righteousness. For those who do not have this fear of the Lord, the awareness that the holy God knows everything—even secrets hidden in the human heart—turns into a cause for terror. See Proverbs 16:2.

14. Note that Proverbs 15:16 says that having a little with the "fear of the Lord" is preferable, while in Proverbs 16:8 having a little with "righteousness" is described similarly. Thus the terms "fear of the Lord" and "righteousness" are used interchangeably.

15. (a) Let volunteers share their responses. (b) Under the Law, God judges both religious and secular activity, even thoughts. In His grace, however, He is delighted with the works and the thoughts of those who have His righteousness by faith. (Recall the answers to questions 6, 8, and 11 above.)

16. The fear of the Lord (recall question 13 above) provides a context in which rebuke and discipline are taken seriously but do not drive a person to despair. Only in this context can a rebuke be "life-giving" (Proverbs 15:31).

Wisdom Builds a Better Life

Proverbs 16:1–22:16

Preparing for the Session

Central Focus

Love for the neighbor, which results from God's love for us, also manifests itself in our work. Based on Proverbs and other biblical books, this lesson focuses on the wise in their work. "Commit to the LORD whatever you do, and your plans will succeed" (Proverbs 16:3).

Objectives

That participants, by the power of the Holy Spirit working through the Word, will

1. be able to describe the teaching of Proverbs about the wise and their work;

2. be prepared for major challenges in faith and life by constant preparation in the form of daily godly living;

3. thank God for what He has done for them, His workmanship, in Christ and appreciate what it means to be a "little Christ" to others;

4. want to act in accord with wisdom in their daily work.

Small-Group Discussion Helps

Day 1 • Proverbs 16

1. The wonder and beauty of human speech is a specific blessing from God for humanity. Although most creatures communicate, none can match the depth of revelation provided by human language. How absolutely fitting that the Messiah adopted the title "Word" to describe Himself and His ministry (John 1:1–14)!

2. He is the Creator and Sustainer. Without Him, no human plan comes to articulation, let alone action.

3. The Lord judges and does not ignore pride and wickedness.

4. (a) Love leads to self-sacrifice and enacts redemption. (b) The love and faithfulness of believers leads to self-sacrifice, which extends God's peace to others too.

Day 2 • Proverbs 17

5. The verse describes how bribes work and how effectively they sway people. This proverb is *not* an endorsement for bribery as a business tactic. For example, see 17:23.

6. Friendship. Part of friendship is consistency in selfless giving.

7. The proverb describes people who draw attention to themselves through needless competition, which stems from pride. They make themselves targets of wrath.

Day 3 • Proverbs 18

8. Friendship and selfishness are mutually exclusive. Therefore, selfishness is poison to friendship. Hence, Proverbs warns against making a pest of oneself with one's friends (25:17); irritating them at ill-considered times, despite intentions that can be quite good (27:14); and trying to gain friends through flattery (29:5).

9. The words of fools are always causing problems, for them as well as for those around them. But the name of the Lord on the lips of the righteous is a power to save them and others.

10. Despite the reality of fair-weather friends in this world, committed friendship is a fine display of love and a great gift of God. Allow for sharing, if there is enough time.

Day 4 • Proverbs 19

11. Notice again the focus on character in Proverbs. It is better to be genuine and poor than to go the way of a fool. Fools are sometimes successful. The implication is that the fool with the perverse lips got rich thereby.

12. Although earthly wealth has the power to turn

heads, Christians need to appreciate true friendship and show compassion for the poor.

13. There are times when Christian concern compels us to go and speak to a fellow believer who "sins against" us (Matthew 18:15). Yet if we were to follow through on every offense that comes along, we'd have time for nothing else. Instead of harboring resentment, in Christ we can overlook wrongs.

14. An undisciplined child is apt to meet the worst possible end: untimely death.

Day 5 • Proverbs 20:1–22:16

15. Even at tender ages, children are moral creatures. Therefore, "a wise son heeds his father's instruction" (Proverbs 13:1), however young he is.

16. In the Old Testament, God showed how serious He was about honor and love of children toward their parents by listing the cursing of parents as punishable by death. On the positive side, "parents are the pride of their children" (Proverbs 17:6).

17. Although it may not be immediately apparent, this passage points out the need for parents to impose discipline early on. A young and correspondingly undisciplined heir will run into problems, as did the prodigal son in Luke 15:11–16.

18. God has arranged the world such that grown children have strength and their parents have gained the respect of others for experience and wisdom. These are the makings of a good complementary relationship. But, of course, better than either strength or experience is knowing the Lord.

19. Although Rehoboam strayed from wisdom in his early reign, he did repent and turn back to God and his father's teachings later in his life.

20. Gifts of tribute were expected from subservient nations and subjects. You typically did not go before your ruler empty-handed. Like any ruler, God holds us accountable for our debts of tribute. We owe Him dearly! Yet, unlike most rulers, He is more than ready to forgive.

The Words of the Wise

Proverbs 22:17–24:34

Preparing for the Session

Central Focus

"Do not let your heart envy sinners, but always be zealous for the fear of the LORD. There is surely a future hope for you, and your hope will not be cut off" (Proverbs 23:17–18).

Objectives

That participants, by the power of the Holy Spirit working through the Word, will

1. understand the relationship between Proverbs and so-called worldly wisdom;

2. recognize God's work through Proverbs and the everyday events of life.

Small-Group Discussion Helps

Day 1 • Proverbs 22:17–23:12

1. The purpose, here as elsewhere in Proverbs, is not mere increase of knowledge, but trust in the Lord. This is indeed the way of the wise.

2. The passage describes the extensive works of wisdom Solomon produced. It does not specifically mention that he collected wise sayings from other nations but shows that he interacted with the wise men of other nations. If Solomon or another collector of proverbs borrowed from other wise writings, this would not undermine the inspiration of Scripture. For example, in Acts 17:28 the apostle Paul cites the Greek poets Epimenides and Aratus in order to make his point about God's creation of humanity. If someone else has already stated a truth well, wouldn't it be wise to cite that person?

3. Although economics have changed since ancient times, some things have not changed: risky investments and debt always carry the threat of financial ruin for those who live by them.

4. (a) Here the Lord takes particular interest in fatherless children. A "Defender" or "Redeemer" was a brother or other close family member who took responsibility for someone who could not act in his or her own behalf. A redeemer helps others out of trouble, buys them back from bondage, and if necessary becomes their substitute. (b) Our Lord Jesus Christ redeemed us from sin and death through His perfect life, death, and resurrection.

Day 2 • Proverbs 23:13–28

5. Although, as Hebrews notes, "no discipline seems pleasant at the time, but painful" (Hebrews 12:11), parents should discipline their children—out of love (compare Proverbs 13:24). Careful discipline is almost the exact opposite of child abuse. It inflicts *temporary* pain for the sake of long-term gain. (By the way, parents themselves do not cease needing discipline. The word translated "instruction" in 23:12 is the same as the word for "discipline" in the next verse, v. 13.)

6. While the relationship between parents and children changes when both get older, it does not cease. If parents are pleased to see evidence of the growing wisdom of their growing children, they are overjoyed to see their adult offspring showing righteousness and wisdom. (And the adult offspring can grow to appreciate the wisdom of their parents all the more.) God forgives our failures in family life just as He forgives other sins. If you struggle with regret or continued family difficulties, take your burdens to the heavenly Father and request His help through His beloved Son.

Day 3 • Proverbs 23:29–24:9

7. God intended the production of wine for our joy and as a relief for those suffering pain. Like any good thing, wine can be abused. God grant us wisdom to use it wisely!

8. It takes a lot of work to build not only physical hous-

es, but also the lives of individuals or families (as noted in the previous lesson). The wise plan and prepare well. They do such work (or "building") with wisdom, understanding, and knowledge, thus translating their wisdom into beneficial effort. As noted in previous lessons, wisdom is multifaceted. It includes skill and technical know-how, "street smarts," and being wise before God by heeding the wisdom in His Word of Law and Gospel (on this last point, see Proverbs 24:14). The wise indeed have great power, although they may look quite humble to the world.

tasks God calls us to as human beings. Find contentment in the basics, which truly are the greatest sources of earthly joy.

Day 4 • Proverbs 24:10–22

9. God has entrusted us with the care of one another. Such care often opens the door to the sharing of the Gospel.

10. God gives His children the strength to keep rising up from adversity and forgiving others. He does this through His Word, which reveals the perfect example of Jesus' life and, most important, His death and resurrection. He also imparts strength through His forgiveness given through the Sacraments, as is reflected in the blessing traditionally given after Holy Communion: "The body and blood of our Lord strengthen and preserve you steadfast in the true faith to life everlasting."

11. The king is God's representative. As such, the king—or other duly constituted authority—acts for the Lord in putting down those who rebel against legitimate authority.

Day 5 • Proverbs 24:23–34

12. Justice must be impartial. Human judges should not acquit the guilty.

13. People love pleasure. They chase fantasies. They lose focus.

14. (a) God called Adam and Eve to be fruitful and multiply, fill and subdue the earth, take care of the Garden of Eden, and care for each other. In other words, he focused them on their families and stewardship of His creation (food in particular). (b) When things don't go well at work, remember these specifics, the primary

Wisdom for Hezekiah's Court

Proverbs 25–29

Preparing for the Session

Central Focus

"When the righteous thrive, the people rejoice; when the wicked rule, the people groan" (Proverbs 29:2).

Objectives

That participants, by the power of the Holy Spirit working through the Word, will

1. understand the court wisdom of this section of Proverbs;

2. be able to describe the general teaching of Proverbs on love for one's neighbor.

3. look to Christ as the power behind their love as well as the pattern for it.

Small-Group Discussion Helps

Day 1 • 2 Kings 16:1–4; 17:1–20; and 18:1–8

1. Ahaz adopted the wicked religious practices of the Northern Kingdom of Israel, including child sacrifice and worship at the high places and beneath trees.

2. The Assyrians defeated the Northern Kingdom and took the Israelites into exile. This happened because the Israelites persisted in idolatry and rebellion against God's covenant. They would not listen to the prophets and repent.

3. Hezekiah returned to the faithful service of God, which David had instituted. He destroyed the idolatrous places of worship and even the bronze serpent cast by Moses, since it had become an object of idolatry. He trusted God, held to the covenant, and instituted a fast, which may be a reference to the festivals of the covenant (e.g., the Day of Atonement included fasting).

Day 2 • Proverbs 25:14

4. Men of Hezekiah, the King of Judah, collected these proverbs of Solomon's.

5. There are many things God has not told us. His ways are past finding out (Romans 11:33–36). But kings search out and discover so they can govern and administer justice. Realizing this responsibility, Solomon asked the Lord for a discerning heart (1 Kings 3:9). The Lord calls you as part of His royal priesthood to learn His ways and declare His praises.

6. Vote the rascals out if you want to have a good government. God grant us wisdom to distinguish between the righteous and the rascals!

Day 3 • Proverbs 25:15–26:5

7. Yet another piece of advice on dealing with kings, this one advises calm and tact, which young people must learn. Well-chosen words can have power even on the most arbitrary and controlling king.

8. These proverbs refer to the effects of having too much of a good thing. Excess leads to resentment.

9. These passages illustrate the wisdom essential to the good administration of justice. Biblical proverbs sometimes appear to be in conflict. They are not truly in conflict, however. Both proverbs are true, but they apply to different situations. It takes wisdom to know when to apply each. They stand next to each other to illustrate an unspoken truth: when working with a fool, you lose if you do say something and you lose if you don't say something. It's a no-win situation.

Day 4 • Read Proverbs 26:6–27:22

10. Here are three snapshots of the lazy person: making excuses (v. 13), remaining nestled in bed (v. 14), sitting at the dinner table, too lazy even to eat his food (v. 15). In other words, the proverb urges us to make no excuses for failure or inaction, rise ready for work, and make the most of our own time.

11. Answers will vary. It should be noted that in God's created order, procrastination brings its own penalties. But failing to meet responsibilities due to procrastination is sinful, thus more serious still. The forgiveness of sins in Christ can help us not to be perfectionists, putting off work until everything is just right. Freed in Christ, we jump into our work.

12. Both open rebuke and open expression of love are vital to healthy family life. Through the Law, our heavenly Father openly rebukes our sins. Through the Gospel, He openly expresses His love for us. He calls us to use this same pattern of Law and Gospel in our family relationships.

. . . .

Day 5 • Proverbs 5; 7

13. Taken literally, this passage describes the benefits of attending to one's own business rather than affairs at court. No one will attend to these tasks more diligently than the owner. The passage may also be speaking on a different level. The prophets regarded the leaders of Israel as "shepherds" of God's people (e.g., Jeremiah 23:1–6; Ezekiel 34). Proverbs 27:23–27 may be urging good government by faithfully caring for the people of the land.

14. The "fear of the Lord" includes a life-long practice of repentance. In contrast to "fear of man," this is a life of blessing. Repentance, faith, and joy are constant companions.

Words from Agur, Lemuel, and a Happy Household

Proverbs 30–31

Preparing for the Session

Central Focus

Love for the neighbor, which results from God's love for us, manifests itself first at home. Based on Proverbs and other biblical books, this lesson focuses on the home life of the wise.

Objectives

That participants, by the power of the Holy Spirit working through the Word, will

1. be able to trace basic biblical connections between home relationships and the Gospel;

2. be able to describe the teaching of Proverbs about the wise and their home life;

3. want to live in accord with wisdom at home.

Small-Group Discussion Helps

Day 1 • Proverbs 30:1–10

1. God alone is the One who accomplishes these things. They illustrate His might in contrast with human impotence. Wisdom recognizes that there will always be more to know about the Almighty.

2. At a time when people like to speculate about "truth for you" and "truth for me," it is good to recall that Scripture texts like this acknowledge that there are such things as lies and falsehoods, which are never treated as anything but bad and undesirable. There *are* absolute truths!

Day 2 • Proverbs 30:11–23

3. Greedy people, and those whom they serve, can never be satisfied. They will leech you of all resources.

4. Answers may vary. Each of the first three things moves or works in a unique way (soaring, slithering, heaving). By comparison there is nothing quite like the bravado and mind games of human courtship. Oh, the things we do for love!

5. A husband and wife *belong* to each other. In view of this, committing adultery is a form of stealing. How ironic that some treat sex and adultery so casually but behave so differently when their money or property is acquired by someone else! Marriage involves mutual care and sharing in a closed relationship. It is special precisely because it belongs to no one else.

Day 3 • Proverbs 30:24–33

6. Self-control. Four kinds of animals are named as examples of self-control, which enables other qualities: diligence in the case of ants, caution in the case of coneys (marmots), cooperation in the case of locusts, and boldness in the case of the lizard.

Day 4 • Proverbs 31:1–9

7. This may be an example of wisdom borrowed from another nation. However, it is possible that Lemuel is a name for one of the Israelite kings or that the word *king* is being used in a broad sense, such as for a tribal leader.

8. Mom tugs on the heartstrings by reminding her son that she carried him in her womb and remained bound to his father. At the time of this teaching she is probably *the* woman in his life. She presses home her counsel before he begins courtship and full leadership. For examples of this, consider the situations of the boy kings Joash (2 Kings 12:1–2; 2 Chronicles 24:1–3) and Josiah (2 Kings 22:1), who would have relied on the guidance of family and counselors early in their reigns.

9. She speaks about the oppressed and the poor, showing herself to be a compassionate person. Perhaps the economic or social conditions under which she speaks made this theme essential. However, these responsibilities are an aspect of the calling of any king.

. . . .

Day 5 • **Read Proverbs 31:10–31**

10. The godly wife is priceless. Character forms the keynote here. Her character accounts for all the other praiseworthy things said about her in this section. And the lynchpin in her character is the fear of the Lord, as the next-to-last verse of the book indicates.

11. As time permits, let volunteers share their responses. The wife of noble character is trustworthy (v. 11), good to her husband (v. 12), industrious, (vv. 13–15, 18–19, 21–24), strong in work and sharp of mind (vv. 16–18, 27). Further, she is generous (v. 20), dignified and hopeful (v. 25), and, of course, wise (v. 26). She is thus worthy of praise from those who know her, especially the members of her family (vv. 28–31). The wife of Proverbs 31 provides positive examples of the many dimensions of marriage.

12. Specific responses will vary, but the general point is that it would make for improvement. Expectations govern so much in relationships that it is difficult to rise above the level of misguided expectations. Encourage participants to reassess their own views on marriage in light of this section.

13. Paul urges a Christian to remain married to a non-Christian spouse rather than seek a divorce. If the non-Christian abandons the marriage (presumably for religious reasons), Paul allows a divorce. Both Peter and Paul offer the hope that God will be at work in the household to sanctify both the spouse and the children. Virtually every congregation has examples of God working through marriage to bring someone to faith.

14. True wisdom comes through "the fear of the Lord." Proverbs is concerned with the "fear of the Lord" in almost its very first (1:7) and last (31:30) verses, as well as throughout. "The fear of the Lord" is an awesome love and respect for God, who made you and has paved the way for your salvation through the life, death, and resurrection of His only Son, Jesus Christ.

LifeLight Expands

LifeLight

Available NOW!

The Bible: An Overview
Genesis, Pt. 1
Genesis, Pt. 2
Exodus, Pt. 1
Exodus, Pt. 2
Wilderness Wanderings
Joshua
Judges
Ruth/Esther
1 & 2 Samuel
Life of David
1 & 2 Kings
1 & 2 Chronicles

Ezra/Nehemiah
Job
Selected Psalms
Proverbs
Ecclesiastes/
   Song of Solomon
Isaiah, Pt. 1
Isaiah, Pt. 2
Jeremiah/Lamentations
Ezekiel
Daniel
Hosea/Joel/Amos
Obadiah/Jonah/Micah
Minor Prophets

Nahum/Habakkuk/
   Zephaniah
Haggai/Zechariah/
   Malachi
Matthew, Pt. 1
Matthew, Pt. 2
Mark
Luke, Pt. 1
Luke, Pt. 2
John, Pt. 1
John, Pt. 2
Acts, Pt. 1
Acts, Pt. 2

Romans, Pt. 1
Romans, Pt. 2
1 Corinthians
2 Corinthians
Galatians/Philippians/
   Colossians
Ephesians/
   1 & 2 Thessalonians
Timothy/Titus/Philemon
Hebrews
James/Jude
1 & 2 Peter
1, 2, 3 John
Revelation

LifeLight Foundations

Baptism
Bible Feasts
Creation, New Creation
The Christian's Mission

End Times
Heaven & Hell
Law & Gospel
Ministry

Miracles
Parables
Prayer
Prophecy

Time between the
   Testaments
Triune God
Worship

CPSIA information can be obtained
at www.ICGtesting.com
Printed in the USA
LVHW06s1955270918
591350LV00015B/53/P